The GAAP Gap

The GAAP Gap

Corporate Disclosure in the Internet Age

Robert E. Litan and
Peter J. Wallison

AEI-Brookings Joint Center for Regulatory Studies

W A S H I N G T O N, D. C.

2000

Available in the United States from the AEI Press, c/o Publisher Resources Inc., 1224 Heil Quaker Blvd., P.O. Box 7001, La Vergne, TN 37086-7001. To order, call 1-800-937-5557. Distributed outside the United States by arrangement with Eurospan, 3 Henrietta Street, London WC2E 8LU, England.

HF 5616 .U5 L58 2000
Litan, Robert E., 1950-
The GAAP gap

Library of Congress Cataloging-in-Publication Data

The GAAP Gap - Corporate Disclosure in the Internet Age/Robert E. Litan and Peter J. Wallison. p. cm.
Includes bibliographical references and index.
ISBN 0-8447-4147-7 (pbk. : alk. paper)
    1. Acounting--Standards--United States. 2. Financial statements--Standards--United States. I. Wallison, Peter J. II. Title.

HF5616.U5 L58 2000
657'.02'1873--dc21   00-050408

1 3 5 7 9 10 8 6 4 2

The AEI Press
Publisher for the American Enterprise Institute
1150 17th Street, N.W.
Washington, D.C. 20036

Printed in the United States of America

Contents

Foreword

This volume is one in a series commissioned by the AEI-Brookings Joint Center for Regulatory Studies to contribute to the continuing debate over regulatory reform. The series will address several fundamental issues in regulation, including the design of effective reforms, the impact of proposed reforms on the public, the political and institutional forces that affect reform, and the effect of globalization on regulation.

Many forms of regulation have grown dramatically in recent decades—especially in the areas of environment, health, and safety. Moreover, expenditures in those areas are likely to continue to grow faster than the rate of government spending. Yet the economic impact of regulation receives much less scrutiny than direct, budgeted government spending. We believe that policymakers need to rectify that imbalance.

The federal government has made substantial progress in reforming economic regulation—principally by deregulating prices and reducing entry barriers in specific industries. For example, over the past two decades consumers have realized major gains from the deregulation of transportation services. Still, policymakers can achieve significant additional gains from fully deregulating other industries, such as telecommunications and electricity.

While deregulating specific industries has led to substantial economywide gains, the steady rise in social regulation—which includes not only environmental, health, and safety standards but many other government-imposed rights and benefits—has had mixed results. Entrepreneurs increasingly face an assortment of employer mandates and legal liabilities that dictate decisions about products, payrolls, and personnel practices. Several scholars have questioned the wisdom of that expansion in social regulation. Some regulations, such as the phaseout of lead in gasoline, have been quite successful, while others have actually led to increased risks. As those regulatory activities grow, so does the need to consider their implications more carefully.

Regulation does not take place in a static environment, as the rapid rise in the use of the Internet suggests. An area of increasing concern is how forces leading to globalization will affect regulation. Living in a more interconnected world will change the way government at all levels can and should regulate the economy. This series will explore a number of issues related to globalization and regulation, such as the design of policies that affect the flow of information in markets and the design of institutions to help protect the environment. We do not take the view that all regulation is bad or that all proposed reforms are good. We should judge regulations by their individual benefits and costs, which have varied widely. Similarly, we should judge reform proposals on the basis of their likely benefits and costs. The important point is that in an era when regulation appears to impose substantial costs in the form of higher consumer prices and lower economic output, carefully weighing the likely benefits and costs of rules and reform proposals is essential for defining an appropriate scope for regulatory activity.

The debates over regulatory policy have often been highly partisan and ill informed. We hope that this series will help illuminate many of the complex issues involved in designing and implementing regulation and regulatory reforms at all levels of government.

ROBERT W. HAHN
ROBERT E. LITAN
AEI-Brookings Joint Center for Regulatory Studies

Acknowledgments

This book reflects the contributions of many people whom we wish to thank at the outset for educating us about the issues surrounding corporate disclosure and acquainting us with some of the most advanced research and thinking in this area. We launched the project by asking specialists in accounting, law, and finance to prepare background papers on various topics. These authors included Joseph McLaughlin, Richard Levich, Katherine Schipper, and Steven Wallman. We are grateful to all these individuals, as well as for the participation of numerous other experts from the private sector in two meetings held at Stanford University and at the Brookings Institution to discuss the issues raised in this monograph. We remain solely responsible for the work that follows, and our views do not necessarily coincide with those of any participants at our meetings.

Finally we want to thank Leah Brooks and Tats Kanenari for their superb research assistance and Kimberly Bliss for helping organize the Stanford and Brookings meetings.

1

The Importance and the Direction of Disclosure

About half of all Americans have investments in the stock market, either directly through the purchase of shares of specific companies or indirectly through one or more mutual funds. Moreover those fortunate to have owned a diversified portfolio of stocks throughout the past two decades have done extraordinarily well. The market as a whole during that period generated investor returns (both dividends and capital gains) of about 15 percent annually. At this rate investors can double the value of their investments about every five years.

The popular media have not ignored the rise in equity prices and have intensified interest in stocks. New cable television channels—such as CNBC and CCNfn—devote much or all of their time to financial news and have created new personalities and stars who are well versed in the lingo of the markets. The Internet has spawned an ever growing number of chat rooms where Net surfers exchange views, news, and gossip about stocks, and increasing numbers of people trade online as well. The bull market in stocks has created a bull market in books about stocks that offer a wide range of views about where the market is headed. The optimist can find his views validated by *Dow 36,000* (Glassman and Hassett 1999). Those who are nervous have probably been made more so by *Irrational Exuberance* (Shiller 2000).

The market has made increasingly wide-reaching impacts on all levels of government and on policymaking. As stock prices have soared, so too have capital gains realized by investors. Higher capi-

1

tal gains translate into larger income tax revenues for federal, state, and some local governments. Indeed credit for a good portion of the improvement in the federal budget outlook over the past several years is attributable to unanticipated increases in receipts from the capital gains tax.

The market is now central to the debate over the future of Social Security. In the mid-1990s the notions of having the federal government invest a portion of the Social Security Trust Fund in equities (as President Clinton has proposed), letting individuals invest a portion of their Social Security contributions themselves in the market (as suggested by presidential candidate George W. Bush and others), and incentivizing individuals to have equity-based accounts on top of their Social Security contributions (as presidential candidate Al Gore has proposed) were on the fringe of political discourse. Today—whatever the outcome of the election—any Social Security reform package will likely include some mechanism to permit individuals to invest in equities for their retirement.

The Federal Reserve Board has also increased its attention to the market. In 1996 Federal Reserve Chairman Alan Greenspan issued his famous warning that investors were displaying "irrational exuberance" in bidding up stock prices. Several years later Greenspan switched course by suggesting that investor behavior may have been justified after all by a surge in productivity growth in the economy. Still he cautioned about a possible downside: the market-created wealth was contributing to excessive demand for consumer goods and thus adding to inflationary risks. Among other factors, this concern appears to have contributed to the steadily higher interest rates that the Fed engineered through much of 2000.

Nonetheless, America's capital markets are still widely and justifiably hailed as the best in the world. The explosive growth of the number of high-tech companies in the 1990s provides visible evidence of why deep and liquid equity markets are so critical. These new companies typically get their start through financing from venture capital (VC) firms, which have attracted increasingly large sums—$50 billion in 1999 and on target to reach close to $100 billion in 2000—from pension funds, university endowments, and wealthy individuals. To these investors, participation in VC funds promises higher returns—albeit with higher risks—than are achievable in the equity markets themselves. But the VC industry could not exist without the equity markets, which enable venture capitalists to turn their investments in new private businesses into liquid shares that can be readily traded when the firms go public.

In short the stock market matters a lot—arguably much more than it ever has—to investors, to consumers, to entrepreneurs, and to policymakers. But what fundamentally determines stock prices? Standard texts on corporate finance provide a ready answer: the price of a company's stock at any given time simply represents a proportionate share of the discounted value of the company's expected future profits. In other words shares of stock are like tickets that entitle their holders to payoffs. What anyone should pay for these tickets will basically depend on three variables: the current profits of the firms issuing the shares, the expected growth of profits, and the rate at which those future profits should be discounted (because a dollar received in the future is not worth as much as a dollar received today). Corporate finance theorists often call the discount rate the *cost of capital,* which consists of a weighted average of the costs of issuing debt and equity.[1]

Investors today appear to take for granted that they have reliable information about the profitability of companies whose stocks they may purchase or sell. Although we question whether this faith is warranted, investors seem to draw confidence from the requirement of the securities laws enacted in the 1930s that publicly held firms issue audited financial statements based on generally accepted accounting principles (GAAP). The principles themselves, which are now developed by the Financial Accounting Standards Board (FASB), provide a standard to permit investors to compare the profits and other financial data of different companies. In addition, companies regularly issue press releases and other reports that help investors form expectations about the growth of profits, as well as about the riskiness of those profits relative to the expected profits of other companies and other financial instruments (information that assists investors in applying an appropriate discount rate). An entire industry and a community—consisting of analysts and news services that interpret financial information and recommend stocks—have grown up around these disclosures.

Treasury Secretary Lawrence Summers (2000) has called the development of GAAP—the standards on which corporate financial statements are based—one of the most important innovations in the history of the capital markets. The reason should be clear. As with any market, the main function of the equity markets is to get prices right so that capital is allocated to its best uses. Capital markets will not send the right signals, however, unless investors have access to accurate information about the financial fortunes of individual companies, as well as general economic trends, on a timely basis. The standardization of financial information that GAAP has enabled has been critical to the production of this information.

It may be easiest to understand why accurate financial information is important when firms raise capital for the first time in an initial public offering (IPO), an important point when savings are channeled to new investments. Even the best information does not protect investors against risks or losses. The spring 2000 plunge in the prices of shares of many dot.com companies that had recently gone public demonstrates the point.

Timely and accurate financial information is also important for markets in shares of well-established companies that may no longer need to acquire new capital but whose stock is traded regularly on organized exchanges. Stock prices in so-called secondary trading provide signals to directors and shareholders of companies of how well management seems to be doing. Not many chief executives of publicly traded companies can count on job security if the price of their company's stock languishes or, even worse, falls steadily over a significant period. Perhaps even more important, many managers and employees of publicly traded firms are paid in stock or options: share prices provide powerful incentives for firms to serve their markets in the most efficient manner possible.

The increasing use of stock and options to motivate employee performance is just one development associated with the New Economy—the rapidly growing importance of high-technology firms and industries. For our purposes, however, we focus on two features associated with the New Economy that have critical—and thus far generally unrecognized—implications for the manner, extent, and timing of information disclosed by publicly traded corporations:

1. the increasing discrepancy between the market values of many corporations and the values of their shareholder equity measured according to their book values in accordance with GAAP

2. the explosive rise of the Internet

We argue that the first development (the increased importance of intangible assets) calls for a fundamental rethinking of the kinds of information that corporations should be disclosing to investors to keep them properly informed about their financial prospects. But it is too early for the government or the body that oversees GAAP, the Financial Accounting Standards Board, to announce by fiat exactly what information would be most useful. Accordingly we advocate instead a period of vigorous experimentation with new measures of performance, which the Securities Exchange Commission (SEC) should encourage.

Meanwhile the second development (the Internet revolution) can be and should be harnessed to provide more timely disclosures to investors. The quarterly pace at which corporations currently provide financial data is strikingly behind the times in the age of the Internet. Ultimately investors will want and companies will supply information on virtually a daily basis, if not more often, with the Internet as the distribution vehicle. The role of accountancy in such a world will dramatically change from one of checking the accuracy of specific numbers to one of monitoring and authenticating the validity of the *processes* by which those numbers are delivered.

In short there is a gap between the GAAP of today and the financial disclosures that can be made and will soon be coming. It is not too soon to begin thinking about how to close the GAAP gap. We have written this book in the hope of starting that process.

The Rise of Intangibles

One defining characteristic of the New Economy is its heavy reliance on information and intangible assets—ideas, often protected by patents, trademarks, or copyrights—rather than physical plant and equipment. The valuations of equities certainly support this view. Baruch Lev, a leading accounting theorist at New York University, points out that the market-to-book ratio for companies in the Standard & Poor's 500 index hovered around one-to-one during the 1977–1983 period: the market value of the equity in these companies was roughly equivalent to their net worth. Since then the market-to-book ratio for the companies in the S&P index has gradually risen to about three-to-one in 1993–1995 and about six-to-one in the late 1990s (Lev 2000, 4). Even with the correction in stock prices in 2000, market-based valuations on average remain many multiples of book values.

The stock market may have been irrationally exuberant since 1983, a condition that would explain the steady rise in valuations. This explanation seems hard to support, however: the market may be irrational for a temporary period, but hardly for seventeen years. It is far more plausible that the markets have been confirming the increased importance of intangible assets, which are not typically reflected in the GAAP-calculated net worth of companies since the expenditures that create them—notably, spending on research and development (which creates patents and other intellectual property), training of employees (which helps to create a loyal work force), and developing and servicing customer bases (which builds customer loyalty)—are generally treated as expenses and not as investments (assets) counted on a company's balance sheet. The rising importance of intangible assets is consistent with the fact that *total factor productivity growth*—or the growth in productivity after taking account of the growth of both labor and capital—has accelerated in the late 1990s (CEA 2000). TFP growth is the gain in output due to advances in knowledge alone rather than to increased inputs.

What does the switch from hard to intangible assets mean for the disclosure of financial information? In a word: everything. The rising disparity between valuations of companies based on share prices and their net worth under conventional accounting conventions suggests that the latter may not be accurately reflecting the underlying values of the enterprises. The techniques that accountants and auditors rely on today to produce or certify financial statements were born in an age when hard assets were the foundations of a company's value. The actual dollars that went into plant, machinery, and real estate accurately reflected value because an equal number of dollars by and large could replicate the productive facilities.

In the New Economy, where information seems to be king, cost is no longer a good indicator of value. A relatively small investment in an idea can produce vast dividends—and a large investment correspondingly can have no value at all. When the assets of major companies are their ability to innovate, the morale and the skills of their employees, the loyalty of their customers, and the temporary efficacy or popularity of their intellectual products, financial statements prepared in the customary manner cease to have much meaning or relevance. That will change only when new measures of these intangible assets are made and routinely disclosed.

The Rise of the Internet

A second key feature of the New Economy is the explosive rise of the Internet, whose economic, social, and political impacts are only beginning to be felt. In the markets the Internet has evidenced its importance in at least two significant ways: through the extraordinary growth of online investing and equities research and through the transformation of the exchanges themselves through the rise of electronic communications networks (ECNs) that match buyers and sellers of stock at fractions of the cost of the prior trading systems.

The Internet also has potentially far-reaching implications for the manner in which investors obtain their information about publicly traded companies. On the demand side, investors accustomed to online trading—and hence virtually instantaneous transactions comparable to those executed by floor brokers—are hungry for a constant flow of information on which to base their trades. Annual audited financial statements clearly do not satisfy this appetite for news, nor do the quarterly financial (unaudited) reports that companies issue. Thus firms are issuing press releases about new products, contracts, and other arrangements on almost a continuous basis (and are required by law to do so).

Meanwhile on the supply side the Internet makes it possible for companies to deliver information to investors, analysts, and other users on virtually a real-time basis. Individuals do not need to watch any specialized cable television networks to find out the latest news about their companies. They simply need to log on to their own computers.

The Net is also becoming a powerful democratizing force for investors. Consider the analysts' conference call with the chief executive of a company, a rite that has become institutionalized when firms announce their earnings results. When only analysts participate, they can take advantage (for themselves or for their firms' clients) of their priority access to particular information that may have a bearing on the stock price. This first-mover advantage can disappear, or at least be weakened significantly, however, when the analysts' calls are broadcast simultaneously on the Internet as required under new financial disclosure rules issued by the SEC in mid-2000. In the markets information is power. When all have access to the same information at the same time, this power is widely—and more fairly—dispersed.

The demand- and supply-side implications of the Internet for corporate disclosure are profound. If companies can use the Net to access information almost constantly and instantaneously—and investors and analysts have a thirst for such information—the obvious result will be much more continuous reporting of financial and business information. Much, if not all, of this information should be designed to help investors better estimate companies' future profitability and relative riskiness so that they can more accurately price companies' true market values.

What's Next?

When traditional methods in our dynamic economy lose their relevance, they are swept away. In their wake new techniques are waiting to be born. So it is with financial and business reporting. In a field long thought to be hidebound and even hostile to innovation, ideas in development could lead to an entirely new system of assessing the value of companies. The only question is whether our laws and regulations—and those who administer and enforce them—have the flexibility and the vision to encourage innovation in this area.

The new methods would use the vast communication capabilities of the Internet and the multiplying power of data processing to decentralize the preparation of financial statements and the interpretation of operating results. In addition to companies preparing their own financial statements—which analysts promptly disaggregate by searching for the "real" values of the various assets and liabilities—firms would report indicators or measures of pertinent activities and perhaps also make raw financial and operating data available on the Internet. This information would be analyzed and interpreted by a large number of competitive analytical groups that would develop as soon as such data existed to be analyzed. Investors too could access the same information.

More broadly, financial reporting must be forward-looking, not only describing assets and liabilities measured at their historical cost but providing as accurate a snapshot as possible of an organization's current operations and likely prospects. In part this can be done through business reporting—releasing nonfinancial data that can be compared with the data of competitors and industry benchmarks.

To be sure, this new approach to disclosure would require agreement on the precise definitions of various indicators and data elements that would be regularly published by companies and that may differ from industry to industry. In the end the availability of much more finely disaggregated financial information would allow investors to gain a better understanding of the underlying values of publicly held enterprises.

In fact, work is under way in many industries on supply chain definitions. A new data-processing idiom known as extensible markup language (XML) allows "tagging" of the multiplicity of information items that are part of the movement of goods in a supply chain. The tags allow software applications of various kinds to dip into this pool of data and extract the information necessary for carrying on business transactions in a common language. When applied to financial and business reporting, this new tagging system will permit more rapid and thorough analysis and benchmarking. Most important, it will enable assessments of company prospects to become user driven, rather than issuer driven.

Why would companies be willing to publish this information and leave themselves exposed to adverse inferences and projections? Their capital costs and the volatility of their share prices should decline as investors gain greater certainty about the values of the companies whose shares they are purchasing. In fact, as we highlight in the next chapter, the history of accounting has involved a continued tug of war between those who fear that too much disclosure will expose a company's secrets to the world and those who believe that the more sunshine a company lets in, the better off investors, and even the companies themselves, will be in the long run. The clear trend has been in the direction of more disclosure, both mandatory and voluntary. We are simply advocating an acceleration of the trend.

What would happen to the accounting profession if certifying financial statements and developing generally accepted accounting principles was no longer its role? As noted earlier in this chapter, accountants would still have a central role in disclosure although their duties would evolve concentrating more on defining the data elements and reporting on the reliability of company disclosures and the integrity of the processes by which company information is developed. In addition, as U.S. and international accounting standards converge, accountants might acquire responsibility for reporting on the reliability of indicators used to measure the intangible assets that increasingly represent the core value of many companies.

But for this purpose a framework is clearly necessary—a new model that would ensure that both financial information and the new nonfinancial indicators needed by investors are of high quality, reliable, and consistent across companies. Regulators could create and enforce such a model. A far better approach, however, would have the new model encouraged by regulators but user and market driven—developed by analysts, corporate financial officers, and the accounting profession.

There is no certainty that the new approaches to the valuation of companies would be better than today's conventions. However, policymakers—particularly the SEC—should be interested in promoting more experimentation in nonconventional disclosures by more companies. The objective after all is better information for investors and markets.

The issues discussed here reach far beyond the headlines of companies whose accounting abuses have been in the news at the end of the twentieth century. An extensive infrastructure of accounting practices and regulatory enforcement guidelines, as well as legal liability standards, is already in place to handle such situations and to deter their frequent recurrence. Similarly the issues addressed in this book remain salient whether or not the equities exchanges (principally the New York Stock Exchange and NASDAQ) and the SEC embrace international accounting standards being refined by the International Accounting Standards Commission (IASC) or continue to stick with U.S.-developed generally accepted accounting principles. Instead, we consider what types of information under any accounting standard would be most likely of interest to investors today and in the near future and how often this information should be disclosed.

Plan of This Book

The thesis of this book is that the rise of the New Economy has generated the need for a new system of corporate disclosure. To explain why, chapter 2 traces the historical roots of the existing system of disclosure, including the development of modern accounting standards. Avoiding a bog of details of accounting theory and practice, we paint a broad picture of who now sets corporate disclosure standards—accounting standards in particular—and what legal structure governs the system.

Chapter 3 then outlines why the move toward a knowledge-based economy—symbolized by the increasing discrepancies between book and market values of companies—poses a fundamental challenge to the current system of corporate disclosure. We discuss both the demands by investors for different kinds of forward-looking information to enable equity markets to set prices of stocks better and the responses of some cutting-edge companies to these demands.

The last two chapters lay out our vision of how corporate disclosure may—and should—evolve in the next few years. As mentioned, we do not believe that the SEC or other regulatory bodies should dictate a one-size-fits-all approach for all companies. Market developments and investor needs are too fluid—and uncertain—for us or any regulatory body to set down in stone an entirely new system of mandated disclosure that is intended for all time.

Instead, government regulators should facilitate and encourage the private sector to establish its own new rules and practices. A virtuous cycle in disclosure should exist in such an environment. Companies at the cutting edge of providing access to information about themselves should reap a cost-of-capital advantage relative to companies that are not so forthcoming. Given the opportunity, markets should enable good disclosure practices to drive out bad—Gresham's law in reverse—without the need for excessive regulatory intrusion or securities litigation.

We are not advocating that the cost-based accounting standards, developed and gradually refined by the Financial Accounting Standards Board, be abandoned. These standards serve an important purpose: they represent the best possible thinking about how the treatment of the types of assets on which they are based—physical and financial assets in particular—should be reflected in financial statements. At the same time we are skeptical that a top-down process of mandatory standards is best suited for fashioning widely accepted practices. For that task the market, encouraged and facilitated by policymakers, is likely to provide the best answers, especially in the current environment of rapid change.

2

A Backward Look at Disclosure Practices and Conventions

Before exploring why the current system of corporate disclosure is increasingly outmoded, it is important to know its origins. A brief discussion of this history is significant because it illustrates well how institutions and practices, backed up by legal rules and developed in previous eras, grew out of the economic circumstances of those times. By implication, therefore, when times change, new thinking about those same practices and institutions is appropriate.

We address several topics in this chapter. We begin with a brief review of the origin of modern accounting standards. We focus on accounting standards because they are the lingua franca of business and because the financial information that companies now report is based on conformance with those standards.

We then outline the legal foundations of the current system of disclosure, which is largely centered around financial information, and proceed naturally to the important question of who sets accounting standards. As business has become more global, a struggle has emerged over which accounting standards should prevail. Observations on the limits of current financial and business reporting set up the analysis and recommendations in succeeding chapters.

U.S. Accounting Standards

Modern accounting is based on the system of double-entry bookkeeping: the notion that every transaction is composed of two parts, a debit (an account that receives funds) and a credit (an account that provides funds).[1] Although some historians trace the origins of the double-entry system to the Romans two thousand years ago, treatises on the subject did not appear until the fifteenth century in Europe. Bookkeeping practices were apparently well established by the nineteenth century in the United States; railroads appeared to be among the first enterprises that made their financial status known to interested readers of business publications. They were driven to do so, as are corporations to this day, by the need to raise capital: to convince investors in their bonds, in particular, that corporate operations could generate enough income to service the interest and repay the principal when it was due.

But financial information is useful only to the extent that it is prepared according to some standard criteria or according to standards that can be verified as accurately representing the transactions that underlie the information. Otherwise investors or lenders cannot assess the risks of handing their funds to specific companies whose founders and managers they are unlikely to know. Perhaps the essential element of capitalism is the supply of capital from individuals and increasingly institutions with no personal connections to the companies that require the funds. A trustworthy set of accounts— and one that allows financial performance of different firms to be compared—is the minimum requirement to enable this transfer of funds from savers to investors to occur.

Accounting standards—practices, to be more precise—developed on their own in the United States and elsewhere through traditions established by generations of entrepreneurs, bookkeepers, and banks. One writer observed that by the late-seventeenth century double-entry bookkeeping "seems to have become the centerpiece in the education of young men and women in the trading classes" (Hunt 1989, 155). No government body had ordered the production of those methods or the system of accounts. Until relatively recently, accounting conventions evolved somewhat the way common law did—through natural evolution, the exposition by various text authors teaching in proprietary trade schools (accounting was not officially taught at the college level until the founding of the

Wharton School of Finance at the University of Pennsylvania in the late 1900s), and communication about those conventions among practitioners and businesses.

At the same time mistrust of financial information has a long lineage, dating at least from the failure of the South Sea Company in 1720 and similar spectacular business failures in the United States throughout the nineteenth century. Some of those who attracted funds were unscrupulous and secretive. They did not want the investors to know what had been done with their money, nor did some businesses or their owners have any intention of honoring the terms of the contracts—whether in the form of bonds or equity—under which the money was made available. The presence of such rogues gradually stimulated the demand for the accounting profession, those trained individuals who would audit companies' financial records, attesting to their accuracy and reliability, in order to provide a measure of assurance to outsiders who were willing to finance them. Companies themselves, however secretive some may have wanted to be with their financial records, also had clear incentives to submit to the auditors because doing so enabled them to attract investors at lower cost. This tension between the desire of owners and managers to maintain secrets and their need to attract funds at the lowest cost is ever present in a capitalist economy. But over time this conflict has been resolved gradually in favor of more, rather than less, disclosure.

Standards emerge in different ways in a market economy. In some cases they develop through the cooperative efforts of experts in the same field or industry, often formalized through a single body. For example, Underwriters Laboratories sets standards for various appliances and pieces of equipment. In other cases standards develop because one company or system becomes so popular that a single standard emerges (the VHS format for videorecorders or the Microsoft Windows operating system for personal computers). Similarly, independent organizations, such as J. D. Power (in the case of automobiles) and Consumer's Reports (in the case of consumer products in general), can gain sufficient public acceptance that their evaluations become the equivalent of standards by which companies and their products and services are judged. Finally, government sometimes imposes standards, as it does today for the environment, automobiles, food safety, and worker safety. The conventional explanation for government involvement in setting standards is the need for government to rectify a market failure, which comes about when private parties have insufficient incentives to account on their own for the full social impacts of their activities.

However, government did not initially become involved in accounting and financial disclosure because of a market failure in information.[2] The origins were quite different and somewhat accidental. In 1887 Congress created the Interstate Commerce Commission to control the rates charged by the railroads, which were then viewed as having an undesirable degree of market power. The ICC was told to limit railroads to rates no higher than necessary to earn a fair return on their capital. How was the public to know what return was fair? To answer that question, the ICC set standards for measuring expenses and required the railroads to disclose the results publicly. Ironically the same industry that began publishing its financial information several decades earlier to attract capital later became the guinea pig for government-mandated disclosure.

The close tie between the origins of mandated financial disclosure in the United States and the rise of the railroad industry had another important feature. Railroads are one of many different types of firms born in the industrial era with earnings generated by the use of physical assets: in this case railroad track and the trains themselves (rolling stock). A key issue then was accounting for the annual purchase of such equipment as an asset or as an expense. Accountants answered with the custom observed to this day: recording the purchase price of the equipment or the tracks as an asset, which was then depreciated at some rate over subsequent years. Depreciation was a way of charging some portion of the acquisition cost of the physical structures or equipment against earnings each year, rather than treating the entire up-front cost as an expense in the year of purchase. Indeed the accounting literature of the late nineteenth century not only contained numerous references to depreciation but was more broadly oriented almost totally toward the measurement of the assets of companies, with earnings treated more or less as an afterthought. The preoccupation with assets rather than earnings grew out of the following accounting identity: assets equals liabilities plus net worth—a concept credited to and popularized by Charles Sprague, whose *Philosophy of Accounts* published in 1908 was the best-known accounting text of its time.

Railroad accounting that became standardized through government fiat proved the exception rather than the rule. In no other sectors of the economy were accounting standards well established. Accountants valued their independence and stoutly and repeatedly resisted prodding by government to establish uniform procedures for preparing and auditing financial statements. Uniformity was viewed as the enemy of discretion and judgment, qualities for which accountants thought they were paid. The profession vigorously fought an early attempt by one of its early organizations—the American Institute of Accountants (AIA)—to codify uniform auditing standards in 1917 and continued to resist similar efforts even after the depression.

Nonetheless government pressure for financial disclosure by companies helped launch accounting as a profession by creating the demand for independent accountants, specifically for auditors. In 1898 an industrial commission appointed by Congress to investigate the impact of business combinations on the U.S. economy recommended that the trusts be required to publish their accounts on a regular basis. Not by coincidence, the following year the New York Stock Exchange first required companies listing their shares on the exchange to issue regular financial statements. In 1903 the Department of Commerce established a Bureau of Corporations, which petitioned Congress annually over a twelve-year period for authority to inspect corporate financial records to ensure their accuracy. Such authority was never granted. The enactment of the federal income tax in 1913 boosted the demand for accounting services, although accounting for tax treatment almost from the beginning diverged from the way accountants tracked the performance of companies for internal and external purposes.

The emergence of accounting as a profession was both symbolized and accelerated by the formation of professional accounting societies through which members exchanged methods of practice—and also restricted entry into the field. In 1896 New York became the first state to enact a certified public accountants law, which was enacted only after it was amended, in deference to British chartered accountants, to include not only U.S. citizens but also individuals who intended to become citizens. By the mid-1920s virtually all states had CPA laws that required new accountants to pass examinations and experience periods of apprenticeships.

Origins of the Current Legal Framework

As it did in so many other ways, the Great Depression marked a watershed in the role of government in the U.S. economy. The stock market crash of 1929 that helped trigger the depression also exposed the unscrupulous and often fraudulent nature of the financial disclosures of firms that issued stock or bonds. By implication blame spread to the accounting profession.

Congress and the Roosevelt administration responded by enacting (and signing into law) the Securities Act of 1933 and the Securities and Exchange Act of 1934. These two statutes have since formed the legal basis of disclosure policy: establishing duties of disclosure by firms when they first register to sell their stock and at regular intervals thereafter, providing penalties for the failure to carry out these duties, and creating a new agency—the Securities and Exchange Commission—to enforce the rules.[3] The 1934 act in particular gave the SEC the authority to set accounting standards or to delegate that authority to accounting professionals with a right to intervene if the commission found it necessary and appropriate to do so.

The commission eventually chose the latter course, but only after much prodding of the accounting profession, which continued to resist efforts to establish uniform methods of reporting and auditing. The accounting bodies even resisted calls for standards by the New York Stock Exchange following the 1929 crash. Two arguments were advanced: there was no single right way to prepare financial records (each company with the assistance of its accountants had to make that decision) and different users wanted different types of information. Interestingly, similar arguments can be made today although there is a need for some standardization in how information-production processes are audited and how specific types of accounts are defined.

Not until 1938 was the SEC successful in persuading the AIA (the predecessor to the current American Institute of Certified Public Accountants, or AICPA) that uniform accounting standards—as they related to the presentation of financial reports—were necessary to provide useful information to investors. In a long process stretching over several decades, professional accounting bodies gradually produced such standards, today known as generally accepted accounting principles (GAAP). The process began with research reports on specific topics by working bodies and would follow (often after extensive public comment) with accounting releases or bulletins that were meant to govern practice. Whereas the focus before the depression was on asset measurement, the principal focus thereafter was on the proper measurement of earnings.

The Roosevelt administration did not think this was an idle exercise. In 1939 Undersecretary of Commerce Edward Noble told the AIA that the major problem then confronting policymakers was stimulating private investment and that a roadblock to achieving that objective was investor uncertainty about the valuation of companies. Accounting standards were viewed as instrumental in reducing that uncertainty and thus in encouraging the investment that the administration believed was necessary to sustain economic recovery from the depression (a process that would not be complete until World War II provided a huge stimulus to aggregate demand). Meanwhile the SEC stood in the wings and threatened to set standards itself if the accountants did not follow through.

SEC regulations under the 1933 and 1934 securities acts compel disclosure of more than just financial data, presented in the now familiar income and balance sheets in companies' quarterly and annual reports. The periodic reports must also contain a thorough discussion of management's discussion and analysis of financial condition. These MD&As are supposed to set forth the companies' goals, plans, and activities that are material to their prospects. All reports are subject to review by the SEC staff, who can require revisions or amendments.

In theory the required disclosures under the securities laws are aimed at enhancing the investing public's knowledge about the financial condition and prospects of publicly held companies. In reality few amateur investors bother to read the reports. The required disclosures are designed primarily for professional investors, analysts employed by both securities firms (sell-side analysts), and institutional investors, such as mutual funds (buy-side analysts). The investing public looks to these intermediaries to help guide their financial decisions or in the case of mutual funds to implement them.

Who Sets Standards Today?

From 1959 to 1973 the Accounting Principles Board of the AIA—which later became the AICPA—set accounting standards. The APB became embroiled during the 1960s in a dispute over accounting for investment tax credits under the federal income tax code. Enough practitioners believed that APB prestige was diminished in the process that AICPA formed a committee to recommend a new system for developing accounting standards. The result was the establishment in 1974 of the Financial Accounting Standards Board, a body of seven permanent members located in Stamford, Connecticut, that continues to oversee the refinement of GAAP.

The FASB does its work much as the APB before it but in more of a public fishbowl. The FASB not only sets its own agenda for changes or updates to GAAP but also takes cues from the SEC. Before publishing proposed rules, the FASB conducts thorough research and after publication solicits public comment. In some cases the issues addressed can attract wide interest outside the professional accounting community. Recent examples of such hot topics include the board's initial proposals to require companies issuing employee stock options to record them as an expense when they are issued rather than when they are exercised; the proposal to require financial institutions to mark their assets and liabilities to market; the impending rule relating to the accounting treatment for financial derivatives; and most recently the proposal to require companies participating in mergers to record them only through the purchase method. That method requires revaluing the acquired company's assets and liabilities at the time of the merger; its opposite, the pooling-of-interests method, allows the merging companies simply to combine their existing balance sheets, both accounted for at historical cost. In each case, elements within the corporate community—the high-tech and financial sectors in particular—have voiced strong concerns that members of Congress have endorsed, especially those on the committees that oversee the SEC. The resulting significant modifications or total revisions of FASB proposals indicate how politically sensitive the development of common accounting standards can be.

Meanwhile the globalization of economic activity has generated interest throughout the world in a body of internationally accepted accounting principles or a set of standards that would allow easy comparison of the financial performance of firms headquartered in different countries. When investors can make such apples-to-apples comparisons, funds should be more efficiently allocated across national borders. International accounting standards do exist because of the hard work of the International Accounting Standards Committee, a body of national accounting associations initially formed in 1973. The work of the IASC has been accelerated by the impetus provided by another international body, the International Organization of Securities Commissioners.

The use of international accounting standards—in lieu of GAAP or alongside it—has proved as politically charged as many accounting issues with which FASB has wrestled in a purely domestic context. Although most of the world's stock exchanges, including those in Europe, Singapore, Australia, and Japan, have accepted IASC standards, two exceptions stand out: Canada and the United States. The SEC continues to require all publicly held companies to use GAAP but permits foreign issuers whose stocks are listed on U.S.-based exchanges to reconcile their statements prepared under IASC standards to GAAP. The SEC has not allowed either domestic or foreign companies whose shares are traded in this country to base their financial reports on IASC in lieu of GAAP, largely because the commission has viewed the IASC standards as weaker than GAAP. Although this view has been contested—there is evidence that financial statements prepared under the two sets of principles do not often result in major differences—the SEC will continue to have the final word at least in this country if and when companies will be allowed or even required to report according to IASC standards.[4]

Limits of Reported Financial Data

Without any denigration of the importance of financial statements, these statements are essentially historical documents. They tell readers (who must have some accounting training if they are to have any understanding of them at all) how companies have performed, not how well they are likely to—except to the extent that past performance can provide some clues to future performance.

Companies also have incentives to provide information about their prospects with respect both to their earnings growth and to their risks in achieving that growth. Other things being equal, companies with wider fluctuations in earnings are typically judged by the market to be riskier investment vehicles and thus carry a higher risk premium than companies with more stable earnings experiences. Higher risk premiums mean higher discount rates, which translate into lower stock prices relative to earnings. At the same time the market rewards growth. Companies with better growth prospects carry larger price-earnings multiples than firms with more limited opportunities for growth.

Two powerful forces work in the other direction, that is, against disclosure. One is the fear often expressed by some companies about disclosing corporate secrets. This fear has been repeated again and again over the past century. It was one of the main reasons why companies were initially hesitant about disclosing any financial information about themselves at all. Over time the cost-of-capital advantages of openness have been winning out. More disclosure, rather than less, has been the direction in which standards-setting bodies are moving and where investors have wanted the process to move. As discussed in chapter 3, the Internet will accelerate the trend toward openness, both because it enables more information to be supplied to investors on a much more rapid basis and because it fuels the appetite of investors for such information. In a sense the Internet is a true field of dreams for those concerned about corporate disclosure. Companies and investors are increasingly coming around to changing how they conduct business and also how they report on that process. And they are doing so in their self-interest: to lower their cost of capital.[5]

The second factor inhibiting more complete disclosure about factors affecting a company's prospects is more problematic: the threat of liability facing companies, officers and directors, and their accountants under both federal and state securities laws for misleading statements. The accounting profession in particular has become well acquainted with the liability laws, especially during the savings and loan crisis, when virtually all major firms were hit with lawsuits. Accounting firms, along with their clients, have also been the object of lawsuits aimed at companies that have suddenly reported unanticipated bad news.[6]

In 1995 Congress enacted the Private Securities Litigation Reform Act, which has made it more difficult for plaintiffs to sue public companies for statements or omissions in connection with their mandated public reports. The 1995 act provided public companies with various safe harbors to insulate them from liability when making certain forward-looking statements.

In practice these safe harbors come into play only when companies surround any forward-looking discussions in their annual reports and other public releases with standard disclaimers and other legal formulas. As a result, the forward-looking components of the MD&A sections of annual reports tend to be discounted by professional analysts, who act as interpreters for all but the most sophisticated investors.

Meanwhile the financial statements that companies release are of limited value for either analysts or investors in forecasting the prospects of companies. Analysts and professional investors increasingly are looking past or ignoring the aggregate presentation of financial data in financial statements and are instead pulling the statements apart or reaggregating them to provide more accurate reflections of a company's worth. Simple examples include adjustments to the income statement to derive cash flow, often measured in relation to some balance sheet figures. Others may attempt to adjust for expenses related to stock options (even though GAAP does not require it) or to impute goodwill in connection with mergers that may have been accounted for by the pooling method. Financial statements—even if prepared according to the current market values of assets and liabilities, as many academic scholars have urged—are not as revealing as measures of the risk exposure of institutions to changes in interest rates. A bank, insurance company, or securities firm may look fine under current macroeconomic assumptions but may quickly look different when these conditions change, as the spectacular near-failure of Long-Term Capital Management demonstrated in the fall of 1998.

While accounting bodies, members of Congress, and corporate interests spend much time arguing about particular rules to be changed or included in GAAP, such debates may be less relevant to analysts and sophisticated investors. These professionals want the raw material that makes up the aggregated financial statements so that they can perform their own analyses of companies. These investors also may want various measures, financial or otherwise, that financial statements do not include but may be far more revealing about a company's prospects—such as the costs of acquiring new customers, measures of employee satisfaction, and managerial capability.

The current standards-based financial reporting system is not well equipped to meet these demands, although it seems to have performed well in generating information on physical and financial assets. But the existing process seems less than ideally equipped for the assets that are driving valuation in today's economy: knowledge-based intellectual property, employee morale and competence, and customer loyalty. Standards that emerge out of extensive deliberations, whether of national or international experts, are inevitably slow to adapt to changing circumstances. Moreover, although accounting standards are not promulgated without input from the public, they are also subject to outside—often political—influences that may be coincident with the interests of investors.

The current standard-setting process is fundamentally antithetical to the culture and the possibilities of the Internet. In the world of the Net, standard setting is a bottom-up process, perhaps best illustrated by the success of the Linux operating system. Linux is open to the worldwide community of computer experts who constantly modify and improve the system. No Linux board debates and vets these changes, which are accepted or rejected by the computer-using community. The standards are user driven.

As the following chapters discuss, we can see the emergence of a similar model for corporate disclosure. The key is to provide the investing public—and more specifically the analyst community that acts as a crucial information intermediary—with sufficient raw data about companies so that they can produce the reports, aggregated in various fashions, that investors find most useful.

3

Corporate Disclosure in the Knowledge Economy

The large discrepancy between balance-sheet net worth and market capitalizationof many public companies may have several explanations. High levels of speculation and changes in the degree of risk that investors see in equity securities are two commonly cited factors. However, neither seems significant enough to explain the extraordinary gap between the values that investors see in listed companies and the balance-sheet values that their financial statements present.[1]

A more powerful and far-reaching explanation may lie in the inadequacy of current financial statements. As noted in chapter 2, today's financial statements were developed in an era in which hard, tangible assets—land, equipment, bricks and mortar, tracks and inventory—were the sources of value. These things were necessary to make and transport goods, and the production of goods was the essence of economic growth.

In today's economy, however, companies do not necessarily create value by creating or using things. Companies create value through the use and development of intangibles—assets that one cannot touch or see—such as innovation, employee skill and imagination, customer loyalty, contractual relationships with suppliers and distributors, and better communications internally and externally. These intangible assets, including trademarks, know-how, patents, software, brands, research and development, strategic alliances, and product differentiation, constitute approximately 80 percent of the value of the S&P 500.[2] If the current financial

26

accounting system cannot effectively measure such assets—and apparently it cannot—we are left without a satisfactory way of assessing and communicating the value that companies create.[3]

This vacuum has serious implications for the health of the U.S. economy and the economies of all other developed nations, where a similar evolution from tangible to intangible assets is occurring. The stakes are relatively high. Without an effective means of measuring and communicating intangible values, poorly informed investors could perceive themselves at greater risk—a perception that could translate in turn into higher degrees of volatility, higher capital costs, and less efficient allocation of capital.

Recognizing this problem, the Organization for Economic Cooperation and Development (OECD) has for several years been sponsoring a program to develop indicators and measures that would supplement conventional financial reporting.[4] The program has attracted considerable attention in Europe but has received relatively little official support or interest in the United States. The question for U.S. policymakers is whether it is prudent to continue to rely solely on conventional accounting statements when there is compelling evidence that they are inadequate—by themselves—to inform investors adequately in an economy based on intangible assets.

Intangible Assets

Neither the term *information age* nor *postindustrial economy* fully captures today's dramatic changes. The developing economy is surely postindustrial in the sense that the main drivers of value are not the large factories, assembly lines, or blue collars that are brought to mind by the term *industry*. But neither is the economy based *solely* on information—unless the term is used in the broadest sense to encompass anything that can be communicated.

A more accurate description would be the *knowledge economy*, reflecting the fact that the key driver of value for many of the fastest-growing companies in the financial and commercial world is what is known—by management, employees, customers, suppliers, contractors, affiliates, and investors. But what is known is a great deal different from what can be manufactured, shipped, insured, broken, repaired, and worn out. These tangible things have a cost that bears a strong relationship to their value since they can generally be replicated for the same number of dollars.

The same relationship does not exist for knowledge. Acquiring or inculcating knowledge has a cost and can be valued in that sense, but if it is lost—say, through the loss of an employee who had specialized knowledge—it probably cannot be replaced immediately or perhaps at all at the original cost.[5]

More important for financial accounting perhaps is the fact that the value of knowledge clearly has little relationship to its cost. A research scientist's ability to understand the vulnerabilities of a virus or a chip designer's skill at miniaturizing an integrated circuit—although both were clearly acquired at a cost—cannot be valued by referring to the cost of the scientist's education or the designer's experience. Similarly and somewhat more abstractly, a company that outsources the goods or services that it sells—that is, relies on others through contractual relationships to serve its customers—derives value from the quality of and its ability to administer these relationships. The actual cost of these relationships and the skills involved in their administration is not an index of their value.

Thus we encounter the problem of accounting for intangibles in the knowledge economy. Unlike the cost of tangible assets, the cost of intangibles—in both the Old and the New Economy—is virtually useless in establishing accounting values. Although this observation may seem like common sense, the consequences for financial accounting are profound.

Financial accounting, as developed to measure the productivity and profitability of manufacturing, transportation, and commercial firms, depends vitally on the accuracy of cost as an index of value. In traditional accounting, the value placed on assets is based on their cost less an amount for their depreciation over time. This approach is conservative, since it avoids the subjectivity associated with placing an appraised value on assets. But even when historical cost is an accurate index of the current value or replacement cost of tangible assets, it has little relationship to the value of intangible assets.

Another purpose of financial accounting—and perhaps a more important one in today's economy—is to produce a reasonable assessment of a company's earnings potential and hence its future value in relation to its risks. Profitability is determined by, among other things, relating revenue to costs. Depreciation in the accounting value of an asset over time is an important method used by accountants to match the costs of production with revenues and allows for an assessment of profitability during a given period. However, without an accurate measurement of initial value or any way of estimating the time that the asset will be useful for the production of income, it becomes extremely difficult to establish the actual profitability of a company through conventional methods of financial accounting. Under such circumstances it is little wonder that price/earnings ratios in the securities markets are puzzling to analysts; the earnings attributable to intangible assets are much less certain than the equivalent results for companies that rely on traditional tangible assets to produce their financial results.

For a large class of companies—the knowledge companies that are the leading edge of growth in today's economy—financial statements based on historical costs are of relatively limited value to investors. But in a knowledge economy the problem of valuation extends even to companies that use conventional tangible assets for the creation of value. Thus, in a paper delivered at the 1999 OECD conference on measuring and reporting intellectual capital, Charles Leadbeater (1999) noted that even conventional products have large intellectual or knowledge components:

> Modern corn is vastly more productive than it was fifty years ago because farmers and plant breeders have developed hybrid seeds more resistant to frost and disease. On some estimates, the average acre of corn now produces 80 percent more usable crop than it did 50 years ago. Modern corn is 80 percent science, 20 percent corn.

Then he continued:

> The knowledge driven economy is about a set of new sources of competitive advantage, particularly the ability to innovate, create new products and exploit new markets, which apply to all industries, high-tech and low-tech, manufacturing and services,

retailing and agriculture. In all industries the key to competitiveness increasingly turns on how people combine, marshal and commercialize their know-how.

Without an accurate measuring rod, investors are left to place their own estimates on companies. The extraordinarily high market valuations that result are a constant source of commentary on the business pages of major newspapers. Many commentators attribute these valuations—which are frequently historically large multiples of earnings, if there are earnings at all—to a kind of market irrationality, as though investors are in thrall to a modern version of the tulip mania that gripped Holland centuries ago. Few of these commentators consider—given the difficulty of establishing the profitability of knowledge companies through traditional accounting methods—how they or anyone else can know what the earnings of these companies actually are.

Under current accounting rules, much of the expense of companies in developing intangible values—such as a brand name, customer loyalty, employee skills, software capabilities, and links to suppliers and complementary websites—are treated as current expenses and not as the development of capital assets. If these costs were capitalized instead of expensed, current earnings might be considerably higher, and earnings might exist where none are now reported.

Our purpose here is not to suggest which approach is the better treatment of these costs—in most cases the answer will depend on too many factors to permit a simple answer—but only to point out that the accounting methods developed in an earlier time for a different kind of company do not lend themselves to easy conclusions concerning such seemingly obvious things as the profitability of companies that acquire their values primarily through the use of intangible assets. Who can know what investors are actually valuing when they pay seemingly sky-high prices—in terms of traditional measures—for equity interests in knowledge companies? Are they looking at current earnings, which might be lower than would be expected if their costs were capitalized, or are they looking at future earnings, which will be higher because these same costs were not capitalized?[6] Conversely, are they looking at current or immediate future earnings at all? Companies that are expanding their intangible assets—their intellectual capital or knowledge capital—might be vastly enhancing their earnings potential without any corresponding increase in their balance-sheet value.

The case of America Online is illustrative. During its early growth AOL spent heavily on customer acquisition and capitalized much of these costs. As a result, it showed earnings for each of the years 1994–1996. The SEC and many in the analyst community complained about this accounting treatment because it permitted the company to show earnings when in fact—if it had expensed these costs—it had none. In 1997 AOL changed its accounting treatment and took a huge charge against earnings for the preceding years—resulting in losses for those years as restated. In 1997, however, even after expensing its customer-acquisition costs, the company showed a profit.

If AOL had not changed its accounting treatment in 1997, anyone looking at the company's financials for the first time would have seen a slow upward progression in profitability from 1994 through 1997. However, because the company decided under pressure to expense its customer-acquisition costs, a reader of its financial statements would have seen losses for three years—suddenly turning to a profit in the fourth.

Which is the better accounting treatment? If AOL had stayed with the capitalization of customer-acquisition costs, its future earnings would have been burdened by the amortization of these capitalized costs. By expensing them, it freed future earnings from this burden and thus looked even more profitable in future years. But the change also meant that the benefits of its earlier spending would not be matched with the expenses incurred to create them.

As it turned out, the better treatment would have been to capitalize customer-acquisition costs. Not only would it have produced a smoother growth in profitability, reflecting the company's growing success, but it would have achieved one of the goals of good financial accounting: match revenues with costs even though they occur in different periods. However, the conclusion might have been otherwise if AOL had turned out to be a failure. While many analysts were complaining about its capitalization of customer-acquisition costs, there was considerable debate about whether these costs would pay off. At that point AOL had serious problems in expanding its physical plant along with its growth in subscribers. A breakdown in its system had left many subscribers without e-mail capability for more than a day, and there was significant doubt that the company would be able to achieve the subscriber numbers that it was projecting. If the skeptics had been right about AOL, expensing its customer-acquisition costs would have been the better and more conservative course because the resulting losses would have warned investors that the company was a gamble.[7]

Ultimately the best accounting treatment for intangibles depends on what value investors place on the quality of the hidden asset that a company is creating with these costs. If the company's brand name is a significant asset because it will contribute to substantial revenues—many multiples of the costs incurred to build this value—then current earnings that are low in relation to its stock price (again by conventional measures) are not particularly important; future earnings—flowing in part from the values built into the company's brand name—will be higher because they will not be reduced by depreciation in the inherent value of this intangible asset. Investors could see and invest in the hidden value imbedded in the intangible assets of knowledge companies, rather than relying on earnings results calculated according to traditional—and less useful—financial accounting methods.

Yet, while investors may be placing high valuations on knowledge companies—regardless of their reported earnings—they are doing so with relatively little information about the quality of the intangibles that these companies are building up internally. This lack of information is perhaps a major cause of the volatility characterizing the securities markets, which has increased in recent years.[8] Investors can hardly be blamed for quick reversals in their estimates of company values when they have so few sources of useful information on the question.

As mentioned, financial statements for companies that rely heavily for their value on intangible assets can be highly uncertain—and sometime highly misleading—guides. As with AOL, a particular accounting treatment may be correct only in retrospect. But still missing is the information that would permit investors and analysts to get a better sense of the quality of a knowledge company's intangible assets, along with the likelihood that it will be able to use these assets profitably.[9]

Lack of information about intangible assets has one other significant effect: it increases the risk premium demanded by investors when they buy a company's securities. Companies that rely on intangibles for a substantial portion of their value probably have a direct interest in improving disclosure and finding ways to inform the market about the true value of these assets.

The Backward Look of Conventional Financial Statements. But the deficiencies of conventional financial statements do not end with their inability to place accurate values on intangible assets, nor do the adverse consequences of the lack of information about companies end with knowledge companies. Financial statements are also inherently backward-looking since they were designed to measure value or profitability at a point in time. A company's financial report tells the investor or the creditor what happened last year, in comparison with previous years. It provides some indication, but not a reliable one, of what investors and creditors really want to know—what the company will do.

The Xerox case, recounted in *The Balanced Scorecard* by Robert S. Kaplan and David P. Norton, vividly demonstrates the weakness of conventional financial statements from the point of view of the investor. According to Kaplan and Norton (1996, 23), while the Xerox patent was in force, the company could lease its machines and collect royalties on every copy. The machines, however, were notoriously unreliable and suffered frequent breakdowns. The company realized that it could take profitable advantage of this deficiency in three ways if it were to sell the machines rather than lease them: through the sale itself, through repair services, and through the additional machines that customers had to buy to keep their operations going while waiting for repairs.

As a result of this strategy, Xerox was highly profitable into the mid-1970s and showed substantially increased earnings year after year. However, the inferior quality of its product had caused Xerox to lose the confidence and goodwill of its customers; when competition for Xerox copiers finally arrived, its customers deserted in droves. The result was a near failure for a company that had once been among the most profitable in the United States.

As the Xerox case shows, financial statements, no matter how accurate, are not sufficient in themselves to answer the question in which investors and creditors are necessarily most interested: How will the company do in the future? Thus, quite apart from the problem of accounting for intangibles, conventional financial statements are inherently deficient for certain purposes because—even in the best of circumstances—they can tell only how the company performed during its last accounting period.

Even this current information, however, is losing its usefulness. In a highly perceptive article published in 1992, Robert K. Elliott (1992, 61) noted that conventional accounting is based on transactions—a product or a service exchanged for cash or a receivable. But the new economy then developing involved many more-complex relationships that conventional accounting did not record at all.

A seller, for example, may provide a buyer with goods, services, and assurances and may receive in return payment now, payment later, and goods or services. This idea captures an aspect of the modern economy that is as true of knowledge companies as it is for companies that create value with tangible assets: important value in contractual relationships does not appear in conventional financial statements. An automobile manufacturer may contract out for its transmissions. If so, the quality of its product may depend importantly on the quality of its supplier and the supplier's assurances and services—items that are not valued in conventional accounting.[10] Not only does this result in a distortion of financial statements, but it also may mislead management—which is forced by conventional accounting to focus on the dollar value of the transaction. In a sense, as Elliott points out, the interests of management and investors are aligned. Both would benefit from a system that more accurately records or reflects the reality—both tangible and intangible—of the transactions that are actually occurring in the economy.

A demonstration of the importance of nonfinancial information to the assessment of a company's value is provided by auditing the conference calls in which companies discuss their financial statements and prospects with analysts. In these calls the overwhelming majority of analyst questions concern nonfinancial information, particularly data that would allow them to project the company's future. For example, in a recent Pepsico conference call, analysts asked about thirty questions of management—only five of those thirty concerned the company's financial statements. Of these, three wanted more refined market segment or regional data on sales. The balance of the questions sought forward-looking information: "How do you see noncarbonated versus carbonated business in the future?" "Do you think gallon growth will match can and bottle growth for the rest of the year?" "What areas are there for analyzing cost structure and margin in the North American snack business?"

Similarly, of forty questions at a recent Exxon Mobil conference call, six concerned financial statements. The rest were asking for information that does not generally appear in financial reports ("Of the employees expected to leave as a result of the merger, how many actually left?") and information about the company's future activities ("Can you be more specific about the capital expense numbers for 2000–2001?"). Other conference calls revealed similar ratios between questions addressed to the financial statements and those concerned with aspects of the company's future that the financial statements do not reflect.

The Problem of Periodicity. Another aspect of conventional financial reports that may mislead both investors and management is the focus of current accounting practice on events during particular periods. Until the advent of the Internet and its unique ability to disseminate information widely and rapidly, problems associated with the periodicity of financial reports could not be resolved. Disseminating in real time some information that is aggregated in financial reports was simply too expensive to be seriously considered.

Management, which must closely monitor a company's operations, does not wait for quarterly reports; reports to management are current and in many cases in real time. Investors, however, are shown only aggregated information for quarterly periods. In the

Internet age it is not clear why this periodicity is necessary. (Chapter 5 covers this issue extensively.) For present purposes, however, it is important to note that the difference between management's real-time knowledge and investors' quarterly information weakens the quality of the information that investors receive and distorts the incentives of management.

SEC Chairman Arthur Levitt has called the consequences of this misalignment of incentives "earnings management." Companies attempt to shape their earnings in each quarter to fit (or slightly exceed) the expectations of the analysts—expectations that management has spent the quarter gently nudging to a manageable number. Regardless of whether the problem of earnings management is as serious as Levitt has suggested, clearly the problem occurs because the underlying real-time data are not made available to investors and analysts but are reported in aggregated form at the end of each quarter.

Perhaps a more important problem, however, is the effect of periodicity on management decisions. In attempting to meet analyst and investor expectations—to avoid surprises—management may make decisions that are not in the best long-term interests of the company. In other words quarterly reporting of information that could be made available in real time sets up a conflict between interests that should ideally be aligned. Robert Elliott (1992, 76) notes that this conflict could cause management to fire people who are necessary for long-term growth instead of closing obsolete plant or equipment:

> It is often stated that American managers suffer from a short-term orientation caused, presumably, by quarterly reporting. However, the problem is not quarterly reporting, it is the difference between external accounting and economic reality (ideally reflected in internal accounting) that gives rise to such acts. If GAAP were a good model of economic success, there would be no harm in managers trying to maximize along a GAAP measurement scale as often as possible. The problem is that GAAP is not a good measurement of the creation of real values.

Thus, while one of the principal deficiencies of conventional financial reporting is its inability to value intangibles in a world in which intangible assets are assuming increasing importance, the backward-looking nature of financial reports and their periodic nature also argue for additional or supplemental corporate reporting that will improve investors' information—and align the incentives of management with those of investors—even for companies that do not rely heavily on intangible assets for the creation of value.

Developments in the Accounting Profession

The accounting profession has recognized that conventional financial reports are of limited usefulness for evaluating business enterprises and at least since the 1990s has been developing ways to improve matters. As early as 1991 the board of directors of the American Institute of Certified Public Accountants appointed a special committee on financial reporting to address such questions in the accounting profession. Earlier, in the fall of 1990, a Wharton symposium on financial reporting and standard setting concluded that "[c]ontinuing on the present course, we believe, will lead to the growing irrelevance of conventional financial reporting in the new age of information" (AICPA 2000a). Similar comments and articles in the accounting literature—in the United States, United Kingdom, and Canada—suggested that financial statements prepared in the traditional form were not only losing their value as indicators of a company's financial position but were failing to address the needs of users. On an official level the chief accountant of the SEC, Walter P. Schuetze, remarked, "We need an … inquiry into the unmet needs of users of financial statements" (AICPA 2000a, app. 4, 1).

The Jenkins Report. With this broad-based commentary in view, the special AICPA committee took on the assignment of determining what information companies should make available for the use of investors, creditors, and analysts and set about surveying these users to determine both their needs and the means by which the accounting profession could satisfy them. The committee report, "Improving Business Reporting—A Customer Focus" (later known as the Jenkins report after the committee's chairman, Edmund L. Jenkins), concluded that company disclosures must be both user driven and forward-looking (AICPA 2000a).

The title of the report, which emphasized business reporting rather than financial reporting, reflected an important change in approach. In effect the committee had concluded that traditional accounting methods and financial statements could not meet the needs of investors and creditors. These needs could be satisfied only by disclosure of information not susceptible to reporting in financial statements.

Generally this information is the data—divided according to each of the company's business segments—that management uses to determine the company's performance but which traditional financial statements do not capture or report. The broadest purpose of such information, according to the committee, is to enable users to forecast for themselves a company's financial future, rather than relying on the forecasts of management. Although the committee avoided specifying exactly what data its business reporting model should contain, it noted the value of such performance measurements as the reject rate for products, sales backlog comparisons over many years, patents obtained annually, and customer satisfaction (AICPA 2000a, chap. 5). This was the first serious attempt by a major accounting group to supplement financial statements with indicators that could add depth and dimension to the estimates of a company's prospects that were otherwise projected or forecast principally from its financial statements.

In a model report prepared by the committee, a hypothetical company—a computer manufacturer named Fauxcom, Inc.—reported (among other indicators) the number of design and installation contracts received, ratio of contracts awarded to number of proposals, market share, average number of employees, average consumption of materials per employee, value of purchased components as a percentage of sales, and product-development lead time. In the committee's view these and other performance measures would provide leading indicators of a company's future, insight into the nature of its business, perspective on its sources of future cash flows, and a picture of management's area of focus—and would provide users with better information on activities that build shareholder value and protect creditors (AICPA 2000a, chap. 5).

Note that Fauxcom was a computer manufacturer with IBM-like aspects; it was selling a tangible product, made with tangible assets, but also had consulting and systems integration segments. In other words the accounting profession had recognized as early as 1991 that financial statements in their traditional form could not provide investors and creditors with the information needed to evaluate business enterprises—even those enterprises that realized most of their value from traditional manufacturing activities. The problem was not only that financial statements failed to provide a basis for establishing a company's value but that financial statements were inherently backward-looking and not designed to provide the information with which investors and creditors could forecast a company's future profitability or soundness.

The effort to bring forward-looking statements into corporate reporting resulted in legislation: the Private Securities Litigation Reform Act of 1995. Congress attempted to incorporate the court-created "bespeaks caution" doctrine by creating a safe harbor for companies to disclose forward-looking information in their prospectuses and annual reports without incurring legal liability. Many observers now regard the effort as unsuccessful. Companies have little incentive to disclose information that might be regarded as misleading in light of future events and seem to have used the safe harbor language to shield themselves from liability in connection with their traditional disclosures rather than disclosing new and useful information to investors.

Since the Jenkins report, developments in the economy have only exacerbated the problem that the report identified. While the findings recommended supplementing traditional financial statements with information that would provide investors and creditors with better ways to evaluate a company's prospects, it did not directly call into question the accuracy of the financial statements themselves. Today it seems clear that—at least for companies that rely on intangible assets for their value—investors need not only the forward-looking and user-driven approaches recommended by the Jenkins report but also measures or indicators that will permit them to acquire a better sense of the values that these companies have created internally. In a recent survey for PriceWaterhouseCoopers, for example, only 22 percent of investors in the United States regarded financial statements as "very useful" in gauging the value of companies (PriceWaterhouseCoopers 1999, 27). If financial statements are not "very useful" in evaluating companies, what information is forming the basis for investors' judgments?

Despite all this, without significant encouragement from the Securities and Exchange Commission, public companies have made relatively little effort to increase disclosure of nonfinancial information that would assist investors to understand company values better. Although individual companies have routinely reported information that goes beyond their financial statements, especially in addressing the questions of analysts, such information differs from company to company in the same industry, is not accompanied by detailed descriptions of how the information was derived, and is not presented in a form that permits comparison between companies.

While this degree of reporting is commendable and should be encouraged, it falls far short of the information necessary for investors to make comparisons among companies. A more robust program would involve the development of indicators and measures that allow a form of cross-company comparisons, similar to the process known as benchmarking.[11] Because investors and analysts can glean useful information from the ad hoc disclosures now being made, a more complete program—coupled with the real-time disclosure of data elements that management itself might use to assess company performance—would help close the gap between what conventional accounting statements report and what investors and analysts need to know. Chapters 4 and 5 cover the constituents of such a reporting system more fully.

The Business Reporting Research Project of the FASB. In 1998 the Financial Accounting Standards Board began a program—the Business Reporting Research Project—to catalogue the disclosures then being made by companies in various industries. Working groups were established to study specific industries. As part of its analysis, each working group developed factors considered "important to informed investment and credit decisions" (FASB 1999). For example, according to the Food Industry Working Group, "these factors were viewed as critical to determining the value of a company from an investment and credit perspective, and came to be referred to as 'value drivers.'" Value drivers in turn were based on the knowledge of the members of each working group concerning the industry involved and their review of the financial information provided by the companies reviewed (FASB nd).

The Food Industry Working Group defined six categories of value drivers: sales growth, margin enhancement, product innovation, product quality, brand effectiveness, and articulation of financial and operational strategies. Each category in turn contained various separate elements. Under margin enhancement were specific kinds of disclosure such as cost control, improvements in productivity, improvements in sales mix, and effectiveness of supply-chain management.

Most of these drivers are not susceptible to numerical presentation. Under sales growth, for example, the Food Industry Working Group included ability and plans to expand internationally, opportunities afforded by alternative distribution channels, nature and extent of licensing agreements, and impact of acquisitions. Clearly such matters would have to be discussed and would inevitably require management to make explicit or implicit forecasts about the likely success of the company's plans.

While these statements would have real value for investors who are trying to understand and evaluate the strategies, resources, and managements of the companies involved, they can be difficult to assess because they reflect value judgments of management and are based on inconsistent criteria that cannot be compared objectively across companies. Statements of this kind should not by any means be discouraged, but a truly effective system of nonfinancial disclosure would have many of the highly successful elements of GAAP reporting: clearly defined and agreed numerical indicators, verified by independent review, and agreed data elements (such as sales of a defined product during a defined period) that would permit comparison across companies.

The business-reporting study, however, turned up apparently strong opposition among companies to setting standards for the disclosure of nonfinancial information. The report stated:

> As noted in the Companies Studied section of the report, a num-
> ber of very large industry leaders declined to participate in the
> study. While no one company came out directly and criticized
> the project, a number of companies contacted expressed con-
> cern over the project becoming a standard setting project which
> would increase [the] required disclosure burden. A number of
> the Task Force members believe that certain current FASB proj-
> ects may be contributing to the unwillingness of companies to
> participate in the study. (FASB 1999)

This statement summarizes a principal reason that there has been so
little progress in the development of a system of nonfinancial disclosure. Companies are concerned that a mandatory system would
increase their costs and legitimately worry about the legal liability
for such disclosures.

As noted in chapter 5, a system of nonfinancial disclosure might
develop through the operation of market incentives alone without
becoming mandatory. If we are correct about the value of such disclosure, companies would find it costly *not* to participate. Furthermore,
the legal liabilities associated with nonfinancial disclosure are closely
related to the type of disclosure. Statements that involve management
judgment are far more likely to produce litigation than agreed and
defined measures or data elements used as indicators.

Accounting Firm Efforts to Implement Jenkins Report. Despite
the somewhat negative view of companies generally, many accounting firms have made efforts to achieve the objectives of the Jenkins
report by illustrating how such programs would work in practice.
Examples are a report by PricewaterhouseCoopers (PwC), *Value
Reporting Forecast 2000,* and *Cracking the Value Code,* by Arthur
Andersen. Both of these recent reports focus—as did the Jenkins
report—on what are called *drivers* of company value or success.
This emphasis reduces the number of indicators or measures that a
company would disclose, but it leaves to management the decision
as to what is important for investors to know.

The PwC report, for example, is described as the firm's "vision of
financial reporting in the twentieth century." It frames the challenge
for corporate disclosure as communicating a company's strategies
for enhancing shareholder values. "Increasingly," the report states,

more sophisticated companies have recognized the shortcomings of the historic financial reporting model as an effective communications tool, and are seeking ways to measure and report on newer and more progressive drivers of value.... In simplest terms, ValueReporting is a comprehensive set of financial and non-financial performance measures and processes, tailored to a company, that provide both historical and predictive indicators of shareholder value. (PricewaterhouseCoopers 1999, 11)

As does the Jenkins report, the PwC document incorporates a hypothetical report of a fictitious company, this time Blueprint, Inc., beginning with a shareholder letter from its chief executive officer (PricewaterhouseCoopers 1999, 13). Significantly the actual business of Blueprint, Inc., is never described, although its CEO provides a full report on its successes and failures during the past year. That Blueprint can be anything from an Old Economy manufacturer to a New Economy knowledge company suggests that the approach might transcend the problem of finding a disclosure system that will work equally well for companies that create value with tangible assets and those that rely on intangibles.

The CEO's report begins with a description of the six financial and four nonfinancial value drivers for the company—those elements responsible for increases (or decreases) in shareholder values. The six financial drivers are sales growth rate, operating profit margin, cash tax rate, working capital to sales, capital expenditure to sales, and cost of capital. The four nonfinancial drivers are process, growth and innovation, people, and customers.

The financial drivers do not appear in conventional financial statements, although they can in some cases be derived from conventional financial data. Success in meeting or exceeding these measures should—other things being equal—result in share appreciation. The nonfinancial indicators cannot be derived from financial reports and generally are not made public by companies if they are used at all. However, the authors of the PwC report believe that disclosure of these measures—or measures like them—will enhance the values that investors see in companies that report success in meeting these standards.

In the customer category the indicators are market share, share of customer spending, customer satisfaction, and product defects. These indicators show (through a survey) how Blueprint is focusing on customer satisfaction with its products, how well it is maintaining its market share against competitors, and the quality of its products as shown by the rate of product defects. In the people category, Blueprint measures and reports employee satisfaction (another survey), the quality of employees measured by qualifications and experience, cultural alignment with markets, and training expenditures.

Under growth and innovation Blueprint measures research and development productivity through the number of patents per R&D dollar, the size of its new product pipeline and the time between development and marketing, the time spent by employees on structured thinking about such things as product innovation, and the relative strength of the company's brands in relation to those of competitors. The control of costs is measured under the process category, which focuses on process costs per transaction, the company's ranking in cross-industry benchmarking studies, efficient use of office space, and outsourcing of non–value-adding activities to others who can perform more efficiently.

These categories and indicators are only suggestive. Making useful judgments about a company from this limited set of data would require knowing more about how the terms in these indicators were defined. Of particular help to investors would be the adoption of these or similar indicators by many other companies similarly situated so that comparisons could be made. Finally Blueprint would have to report changes in the data—good and bad—over a series of years. In the end investors would have to agree that the drivers of value identified by Blueprint's CEO were the most important nonfinancial data about the company.

There is value in most new disclosures. While the development of benchmarking indicators or measures that would permit comparisons among companies would be highly valuable to investors, any nonfinancial data that supplements the financial statements—assuming it is fairly derived and presented—almost surely would be better than none.

Indeed, in a survey conducted by PwC during 1998 and 1999,

investors clearly regarded nonfinancial supplementary data as having an importance almost equal to that of earnings and cash flows in evaluating companies. In the survey 94 percent of investors rated cash flows as "particularly valuable" in making investment decisions, but an equal number cited R&D investment amounts; 92 percent cited earnings, but 90 percent cited market share, capital expenditure, and new product development—three indicators that do not appear in conventional financial statements. Further down the list, substantial majorities cited employee productivity (78 percent), customer retention (72 percent), product quality (72 percent), and customer satisfaction (58 percent) (PricewaterhouseCoopers 1999, 76).

The Arthur Andersen report also focuses on value drivers but is more clearly directed to the uses that management might make of these indicators rather than their value for informing investors. Nevertheless, the report contains a set of illustrative indicators that could be used for both purposes. Keeping in mind the importance of aligning the incentives of management with the interests of investors, it is clear that the authors of the Arthur Andersen report considered that the indicators selected could be used both internally and externally.

In its discussion of indicators, the report points out that

> there is no single set of success factors or key performance indicators (KPIs) that make sense for every business.... AT&T might focus on customer retention as a KPI because of the unique competitive environment of the long-distance communications industry. In contrast, Home Depot might focus more on 'revenue per customer visit' to monitor in-store sales and the overall shopping experience. (Arthur Andersen 2000, 223)

The report then provides an illustrative set of KPIs, arranged into five categories that it calls asset classes: financial, physical, customer, employee and supplier, and organization. The categories are similar to those used by PwC. Each class is then divided into three sectors corresponding to the quantity or value of the asset, the rate of change of the asset, and the efficiency with which the asset is operated to achieve a specific outcome. For example, the asset category of customer is looked at in three ways: as a quantity (num-

ber of customers, market share), as a flow (customer churn), and as
a measure of operational effectiveness (customer satisfaction, revenue per customer). Using indicators in this way, the Arthur
Andersen authors state, "will allow companies, including yours, to
measure tangible and intangible assets at fair value" (Arthur
Andersen 2000, 223).

Renewed Focus on the Intangibles Problem

Meanwhile accounting theorists continued to struggle with the
problem of how to make financial statements for knowledge companies more accurate. In an early draft of his forthcoming
Intangibles, Baruch Lev (2000) details the adverse consequences for
investors and the economy generally of a system in which internally
generated intangibles do not appear on balance sheets. To address
this situation, he proposes three steps:

1. modifying current accounting to provide for the capitalization
   of intangibles under specific circumstances

2. supplementing financial statements with a system of nonfinancial indicators

3. changing the current system of one financial report per period
   to a series of "continuously revised" reports, reflecting the
   gradual resolution of uncertainty

Because Lev believes that accountants' reluctance to capitalize
intangible expenses is attributable to uncertainty about their ulti-
mate value, he recommends that when these values become clear,
past expenses should be capitalized, with a required restatement of
financial reports for prior periods. This approach may involve legal
risks. The point at which intangible assets should be capitalized
entails a judgment by management, and this judgment is subject to
second-guessing in light of later events. To take the previous AOL
example in reverse, assume that the company had been expensing
its customer acquisition costs from 1994 through 1996 and then
reversed its treatment—as Lev proposes—in 1997. In effect losses
during prior periods would become profits, and the 1997 profit
would be enhanced.

In this case investors could reasonably take the company's decision to capitalize its customer acquisition costs as a bullish sign—in effect a statement that management viewed its investments as beginning to bear fruit. Suppose, however, that instead of the success that AOL realized in future years, the company encountered strong competition—perhaps one other better-funded company such as AT&T or Walt Disney successfully attracted the customers who would otherwise have gone to AOL. As a result the company could not expand its customer base as it had projected, and its earnings growth abruptly stalled in 1998. The capitalization of customer-acquisition expenses beginning in 1997 would then have been highly misleading, and a shareholder suit might well have followed.

The solution to the problem of intangibles seems to rest entirely—or even substantially—with changes in how companies treat intangibles in their financial statements. Lev appears to agree with this conclusion because he proposes an additional way through which investors may get a better sense of the value of intangibles than financial statements might provide. Significantly this proposal does not require company managements to make forecasts about the quality of the company's intangible assets.

Lev's proposal is what he calls an innovation index—a set of indicators that would provide investors and others with a way of evaluating a company's success in innovating through research and development. The index would consist of a series of indicators in three categories: inputs, intermediate outputs, and final outputs. Inputs are such things as research and development, customer acquisition, and investment in training. Examples of intermediate outputs are patents, trademarks, and performance measures. Final outputs are such things as revenue from new products and changes in production costs.

The innovation index is not the only set of indicators that would be developed, and the indicators that Lev suggests are not intended to be exhaustive. Instead, the index is simply illustrative of the kinds of information that could be made available by companies to supplement their financial statements and to assist investors, analysts, and creditors in assessing the company's progress in building the value of its intangible assets.

Lev also sets out three criteria for this kind of nonfinancial information:

1. All measures must be quantitative so that they can be presented numerically.

2. They must either be standardized or standardizable, so that they can be compared across firms.

3. They must be relevant to users in the sense that they must have some association with an increase or decrease in the value of the company involved. (2000, 99)

Lev's proposed criteria are important for several reasons. First, because it does not require management to make forecasts—but simply to report numbers with respect to particular indicators—Lev's proposal avoids the problems of legal liability associated with management judgments evaluated in the light of later developments. Second, by requiring that the indicators be numerical and standardizable, Lev's proposal makes possible the development of a disclosure system that can be accessed by analysts and investors over the Internet (chapter 4 discusses the importance of this idea). Finally, in noting that the indicators must be relevant to users, Lev is implicitly adopting an idea that underlay the original Jenkins report: corporate disclosure must be user driven rather than management driven.

It is useful to array developments on corporate disclosure in the accounting profession along a continuum: at one end are early concerns—at the beginning of the 1990s—about the inability of conventional financial statements to provide forward-looking information, and at the other are Professor Lev's concerns at the beginning of the millennium about the inability of conventional accounting methods to provide accurate measures of intangibles. The most recently noted concerns are noteworthy. To ensure the rational allocation of capital, it is necessary to furnish investors with information about the prospects of companies, a basic element of which is the quality and value of the intangible assets that many of these companies—and especially knowledge companies—are building internally.

Development of Performance Measures Elsewhere

There is more to our study, however. The deficiencies of financial statements as measures of a company's progress have become obvious not only to leading accounting practioners and theorists but also to managers themselves. As the Xerox example showed, management as well as investors could be misled by an exclusive focus on the company's financial statements into believing that the company was succeeding when in fact it was failing badly to provide for its future.

This was not simply a rearview-mirror problem; it was also a problem of developing the data that would enable management to predict where the company was headed. In a sense management's interests are fully aligned with investors'; both need more effective measures of a company's progress—its success, or lack of success, in meeting its goals or implementing its strategy. In addition, if management uses indicators or measures that provide this information, wouldn't these same indicators be useful to investors? If so, the disclosure of these indicators might meet the need to supplement conventional accounting statements without imposing the additional costs that many companies fear.

One of the first efforts to address the need for indicators as a management tool was *The Balanced Scorecard,* which outlined a comprehensive approach to managing a company by supplementing conventional financial information with nonfinancial measures of how a company is meeting its goals. The authors, Robert S. Kaplan and David P. Norton, recognize the inadequacy of conventional financial statements as management tools in much the same terms as we have already outlined:

> If intangible assets and company capabilities could be valued within the financial accounting model, organizations that enhanced these assets and capabilities could communicate this improvement to employees, shareholders, creditors, and communities.... Realistically, however, difficulties in placing a reliable financial value on such assets as the new product pipeline; process capabilities; employee skills, motivation, and flexibility; customer loyalty; data bases; and systems will likely preclude them from ever being recognized in organizational balance

sheets. Yet these are the very assets and capabilities that are critical for success in today's and tomorrow's competitive environment. (Kaplan and Norton 1996, 7)

The inadequacy of conventional financial statements for evaluating intangible assets is only part of the problem facing management. The other part is the same as the problem facing investors: the backward-looking character of financial reports.

The Balanced Scorecard retains traditional financial measures. But financial measures tell the story of past events, an adequate story for industrial age companies for which investments in long-term capabilities and customer relationships were not critical for success. These financial measures are inadequate, however, for guiding and evaluating the journey that information age companies must make to create future value through investment in customers, suppliers, employees, processes, technology, and innovation. (Kaplan and Norton 1996, 7)

These deficiencies have led companies surveyed and reported on by Kaplan and Norton to develop management systems that enable corporate managers to communicate company objectives to employees, align activities and decisions with an overall strategy, and assess the success of the strategy in meeting the company's objectives. *The Balanced Scorecard,* generalizing from these efforts, is a framework that shows how a company might translate its strategy into a coherent set of performance measures (Kaplan and Norton 1996, 24).

The performance measures are key elements of *The Balanced Scorecard.* Each company is likely to have unique measures to assess the success of its particular strategy. But Kaplan and Norton note that many measures are common to all companies. These "core" measures address the company's financial objectives, its relationship to its customers, its internal business processes, and its learning and growth objectives.

Financial Measures. Financial measures intended to assess the company's return on investment in specific aspects of its business and the economic value added by its operations do not generally appear in financial statements. Kaplan and Norton note that different companies at different stages of development have different financial objectives. Maximization of cash flow may not be as important to a fledgling company in a growing market as to a mature company in a mature market.

Examples of the measures important to growth companies are revenue from new products, gross margins from new products and services, and percentage of revenues from new customers, market segments, and geographic regions. These measures tend to show whether the company is achieving its growth goals (Kaplan and Norton 1996, 51–54). Similar measures, with a different purpose, might be appropriate for companies focused on sustaining a dominant market position or "harvesting" the results of success in a mature market. The financial measures are tailored to the strategy and objectives of the company and generally are not the same as the financial results reported in conventional financial statements.

Customer Measures. The customer core group includes market share, customer retention, customer acquisition, customer satisfaction, and customer profitability. Market share is not as simple as it may seem. Banks may want to measure their share of a target group's total number of financial transactions; a beverage company, its share of a targeted group's beverage purchases; and a retailer, its share of its customers' total clothing purchases.

Customer retention and loyalty can be measured by percentage growth of business with existing customers. Customer acquisition can be measured by the number of responses to solicitations or the conversion rate at which customers responding to solicitations actually purchase goods or services. Solicitation cost per new customer acquired and new customer revenues per dollar of solicitation cost would also be useful measures. Kaplan and Norton (1996, 67–71) list other measures used by companies to assess customer satisfaction and customer profitability.

Internal Business Process. A company develops this group of measures, according to Kaplan and Norton, after deciding its financial and customer approach and their associated measures. The company's internal business processes and the measures to assess the success in carrying them out are then developed; ideally they should support and derive from the company's choices in the financial and customer sectors.

Kaplan and Norton see these measures falling under three broad categories: innovations, operations, and postsale service. Acknowledging that developing measures for innovation or research and development is difficult, they warn that "difficulty in measuring the conversion of inputs to outputs in R&D should not prevent organizations from specifying objectives and measures for such a critical organizational process" (Kaplan and Norton 1996, 100).

Several companies have developed useful measures of innovation. Hewlett-Packard uses a measure known as breakeven time, or BET. This measures the time for a new product to recover its development costs. The measure has the advantage of communicating to personnel that new products must have market potential, that they must be profitable, and that the time needed for profitability is important. Other measures, such as gross margin from new products, help to assess whether a new product is a breakthrough idea or merely a product extension. Still other measures assess operations and postsale service effectiveness.

Learning and Growth. Measures in this core category attempt to assess employee satisfaction, retention, and productivity. Employee satisfaction is generally considered the driver of employee retention and productivity, as well as the key to customer satisfaction. Employee satisfaction is generally measured with surveys; a number of indicators of employee retention and productivity exist (Kaplan and Norton 1996, 130–32).

Enhancing employee skills and measuring growth in this area are difficult, but many companies have developed measures for this purpose. One example is the strategic job coverage ratio, which tells management the number of employees qualified for specific functions that the company will need. Where the ratio is low, management is signaled to enhance employee skills in the necessary areas or hire additional personnel who have these skills (Kaplan and Norton 1996, 133).

We have discussed *The Balanced Scorecard* in detail not only because it demonstrates that management must go beyond conventional financial statements to get a clear picture of company performance but also because many companies have already begun to develop measures that will accomplish this objective.

It is important to note the similarity between the core categories and measures reported by Kaplan and Norton and the categories in the hypothetical president's letter for Blueprint, Inc., outlined in the PwC document, *ValueReporting* and the Arthur Andersen book, *Cracking the Value Code*. PwC organized the president's report into five categories of drivers of shareholder value: financial, customers, process, growth and innovation, and people. Similarly the Arthur Andersen study used the financial, physical, customer, employee and supplier, and organization categories. Both overlap almost completely with the core measures that Kaplan and Norton found common to the companies studied. This similarity suggests that the same information that management uses to assess the progress of a company may also be usable—with appropriate adjustments—for reporting to shareholders, creditors, and potential investors.

Some companies are doing just this, although their numbers are few. The leader appears to be a Swedish insurance company, Skandia International Insurance Corporation. As early as 1991, Skandia began developing ways to measure its largely intangible assets as a supplement to its conventional accounting statements. In 1994 Skandia published the first of many subsequent annual supplements of this type.

Skandia knew exactly what it was doing and why. In an opening statement its president remarked:

> Commercial enterprises have always been valued according to their financial assets and sales, their real estate holdings, or other tangible assets. These views of the industrial age dominate our perception of business to this day—even though the underlying reality began changing decades ago. Today it is the service sector that stands for dynamism and innovative capacity—where jobs are being created and investment is in high demand. The service sector has few visible assets, however. What price does one assign to creativity, service standards or unique computer systems? Auditors, analysts and accounting people have long lacked instruments and generally accepted norms for accurately valuing service companies and their "intellectual capital." (Skandia 1994, 3)

In the 1994 supplement and in subsequent years, Skandia published a variety of indicators and measures that were used by management to assess the progress of the company and some of its subsidiaries on a variety of fronts. For example, with respect to Skandia's fund manager, SkandiaBanken Fonder, the 1994 supplement contained the following indicators of the company's progress: fund assets/employee, market share, customers lost, administrative expenses/managed assets, cost for administrative error, and competence-development expense/employee. Similar measures and indicators were published for several other subsidiaries. Because this was the first year in which such data were published, there were no time series, but these were published in subsequent years.

In the 1995 supplement the company addressed value creation, especially from operating processes. Measuring value creation is the key to placing a value on knowledge companies. In a preface the company stated:

> A company's value consists of more than what is shown in the traditional income statement and balance sheet. Hidden assets, consisting of the employees' competence, computer systems, work processes, trademarks, customer lists, and so on, are obtaining increasing importance in assessing the value of a company. (Skandia 1995, 4)

The indicators and measures of intellectual capital in the 1995 supplement were arranged into four categories: customer focus, process focus, human focus, and renewal and development focus. Again it is instructive to note the similarity of these categories to those used in *The Balanced Scorecard* for management and control purposes and in the studies produced by PricewaterhouseCoopers and Arthur Andersen as examples of good nonfinancial disclosure to investors.

One of the examples in the 1995 supplement was American Skandia, a subsidiary engaged in brokerage and financial planning in the United States. Recognizing first that "it is important to identify which processes are sources of value creation for the company—currently and prospectively—i.e., core processes, the processes considered to be of strategic importance for American Skandia" (Skandia 1995, 19), the 1995 supplement included measures that were both management tools and intended to give investors and shareholders a sense of the development of the U.S. subsidiary's value creation. These included value added/employee, number of contracts, training expense/employee, change in a company's literacy in information technology (IT), number of contracts/employee, processing time (new contracts), processing time (changes), and premiums from new launches. These measures were displayed in time series 1992–1995.

In a special 1998 report on its efforts to develop human capital, the company disclosed time series for indicators going back four years for each of Skandia's major subsidiaries (Skandia 1998, 21). This report is also noteworthy for its effort to define the components of a company's intangible assets. These the report consolidates under the single heading of intellectual capital (IC):

> IC consists of human capital and structural capital. Structural capital, in turn, consists of customer capital and organizational capital, that is, everything that remains when the employees have gone home, i.e., information systems, databases, IT software, and so on. Organizational capital can be broken down into process capital (value-creating and nonvalue-creating processes), culture, and innovation capital (intangible rights, trademarks, patents, knowledge recipes and business secrets). (Skandia 1998, 4)

Skandia was a pioneer in the effort to identify the sources of what it calls intellectual capital and to provide measures by which viewers outside the company could better assess its value and its future. However, the indicators and measures that Skandia has developed are not uniform across business sectors, are not comparable to those of other companies, and have not been verified for either their probative value or their accuracy.

Chapter 4 considers how the enormous communication potential of the Internet could be used to disseminate a more complete set of indicators than Skandia has thus far developed, how these indicators and measures might grow out of the fertile soil created by the efforts outlined above, and how that would improve the confidence of investors in the valuations they place on companies, the allocation of capital in the economy as a whole, and the functioning of the securities markets.

4

The Way Forward

In their 1999 book, *Performance Drivers*, Nils-Goran Olve, Jan Roy, and Magnus Wetter note that Skandia believes its nonfinancial disclosures have been well received by investors and analysts:

> According to the company, the supplements have attracted considerable interest, even among financial analysts, and are distributed about as widely as the annual report itself. The more detailed view of the company provided by the supplements is appealing to investors who look to long-term sustainability. The risk of divulging too much about the company's intentions is not considered serious.... This kind of accounting reveals the dynamic forces which give the company's stock its market value. It provides both internal and external stakeholders with information that will give them a better understanding—and sooner—of Skandia's future earning capacity. (Olve, Roy, and Wetter 1999, 281–83)

If Skandia is correct, such nonfinancial disclosures could address many problems that the accounting profession and securities market observers have seen in the current financial system. As outlined in chapter 3, these problems include the backward-looking nature of conventional accounting statements and their inability to establish values for knowledge companies or others that rely heavily on intangible assets. These facts have led to the diminishing value of conventional financial statements, the inability of investors to establish satisfactory values for securities, and perhaps the extreme volatility in the securities markets during the past few years.

But too much should not be made of Skandia's disclosures. Their significance comes from demonstrating that measures or indicators used by management could also be used to inform investors. In themselves these measures have deficiencies. For one thing they sample only the company's subsidiaries and do not cover the company as a whole. Moreover, Skandia does not issue detailed descriptions of how the individual measures are derived and what they actually include. More specifically there is no indication whether these measures represent the totality of the indicators used by management of each subsidiary or only a sampling.

Skandia's publication of at least some of its measures—even if they were comprehensive and well defined—also would not solve the problem of periodicity. The measures are published along with the company's annual report. In this sense they suffer from the same deficiency as conventional financial statements: they do not give investors a real-time view of the company even though the Internet makes such a view possible. If Skandia's management actually used the measures to assess the company's performance, they would get the results as the year progressed, not simply at the end of the year.

Olve, Roy, and Wetter point out that companies, in both text and notes to financial statements, have long been furnishing information that amounts to nonfinancial disclosure. The FASB study also reported this activity, as discussed in chapter 3. But are the information and the manner of reporting it satisfactory for informing investors who do not have the special knowledge or expertise of professional analysts? Comparing this information across companies is also difficult, these authors note—since these disclosures are not uniform and may not be consistently applied. Furthermore, there is the question of verifying the facts reported. "This kind of information, if the market is to understand it and feel confident about it, must be relatively compact, use understandable measures, and be possible to verify in some way" (Olve, Roy, and Wetter, 1999, 283).

The three criteria outlined by Baruch Lev—that the measures be quantitatives, standardized, and relevant—are perhaps a more useful way to assess various nonfinancial indicators. Using these criteria, the balance of this chapter considers what form these measures should take and how they might be disseminated and verified.

Quantitative, Standardized, and Relevant Measures

At an early February 2000 meeting with analysts, Amazon.com did an unusual thing—it revealed its customer-acquisition costs, the amount it costs the company to acquire each new customer. Amazon's customer-acquisition costs had been a highly sought data point among analysts but could not be teased out of its financial statements with sufficient precision to provide the basis for a forecast. The market for Amazon's stock was strong at the time, but when the company revealed this figure, it gained more than six points.

A retailer's customer-acquisition costs are an important indicator of its overall success. At any given point the figure can suggest whether the company's marketing program is effective; over time the figure can indicate whether the firm can sustain its earnings growth by attracting new customers at a reasonable cost.

By itself customer-acquisition cost is a relatively weak indicator of future preferences. Several other factors would have to be known before the cost data could be truly indicative, say, of long-term revenue growth. For one thing it might be necessary to know whether the new customers are attracted to all product offerings or only to old ones. At some point old products saturate their potential market, and revenue slows. Attracting customers to new product offerings might suggest that the company's earnings growth is sustainable.

But if customers are attracted to new product offerings, can the company continuously produce new products? To make a judgment about this, one would have to see indicators of the company's ability to produce new products and whether the new product pipeline is rapid enough to sustain the growth rate that seems to be implicit in the stock price.

The Amazon figure for customer-acquisition cost was a companywide number. But Amazon sells more than one product. Its offerings include compact disks, films and music videos, electronics, software, and pool and patio furniture; it holds online auctions; it has expanded outside the United States. A truly useful indicator of likely future performance would provide some idea of the success of each of these ventures in attracting customers. At some point, however, the disclosure of information can be of greater use to competitors than investors (chapter 5 discusses this aspect). Clearly some data on customer-acquisition costs, no matter how general, would be useful. Amazon's format meets the Baruch Lev test: it is quantitative, standardized (or standardizable), and relevant.

Another example is the AOL customer-acquisition effort discussed in chapter 3. In the years 1994–1997 AOL was pursuing a novel and risky strategy for developing its customer base. It sent out free disks at great expense to get potential customers to use its facilities. At the same time it was expanding its server and communications base to accommodate the anticipated new subscribers. The question on the minds of analysts and investors was whether this strategy was working. There was doubt that many customers, once they had signed on, actually did more than take a trial run. If this were true, the company could be headed for disaster; conversely, if a substantial portion of its customers actually stayed on to use the company's facilities regularly, the companys prospects would be bright.

For this reason AOL's disclosure of a customer-retention indicator—say, the regular publication of average revenue from customers who had signed on for the first time within the past month—would probably have been a far more important indicator for investors than the current revenue figures contained in the company's financial statements. It is particularly ironic that the SEC charged the company with misleading investors by capitalizing its customer-acquisition costs when a far more important number—the company's ability to retain the customers being acquired—was not considered significant enough to disclose. Such a measure would certainly have been—in Baruch Lev's terms—quantitative, standardized (or standardizable), and relevant.

Many other indicators or measures of this kind—many of them cited in chapter 3 or used by Skandia—reflect customer loyalty or satisfaction, employee retention, development of employee skills, product defect or return rates, and efficiency in developing new products or in streamlining operations. Management uses many of these measures, as described by Kaplan and Norton in *The Balanced Scorecard,* internally to determine whether a company is meeting its own objectives. For this purpose they have been defined, refined, and standardized so that they provide the most accurate picture possible—given the limitations of all measures.

Olve, Roy, and Wetter note that all measures have limitations, but that does not mean that the measures should not be developed in the first instance:

> Since the measures available are not perfect, may not completely capture the phenomena which interest us, or can be manipulated, their value will surely be questioned. But we do not regard that likelihood as a problem. Good solutions are so often rejected in the search for perfection. Of course we should be looking for the best possible measures, but we should not refrain from choosing measures just because the ones available are less than perfect. (Olve, Roy, and Wetter 1999, 123)

In reality, then, many indicators in current use are both compact and understandable. Their use by management testifies to their usefulness as measures of a company's condition and progress.

Accordingly, management itself uses at least one kind of indicator as a measure to assess the company's progress. The Amazon customer-acquisition cost and the AOL customer-retention factor are this kind of indicator. As measures developed from the company's underlying data, they are summaries of individual transactions but not of the transactions themselves. They would not be costly to prepare and disseminate because the company's management already uses them—or should—to assess its success in meeting its objectives.

But it is also possible to imagine indicators that are not summaries of transactions but are transactions themselves (for example, the advance purchase of a critical raw material), actual management decisions that affect how transactions or assets are treated for financial purposes (the establishment of the projected useful life for a new software product), or indicators of the value of certain assets (the number of research scientists employed by the company).

Although, as far as we are aware, no company makes this kind of data available to outsiders, various technological developments—particularly the Internet and the new extensible markup language (XML) that was developed for use on the Internet—would allow such information ultimately to be made available to investors. The accounting profession, through the AICPA, is engaged in the development of XBRL (extensible business reporting language), which is intended to permit the publication of financial statements on the Internet in a format that will use the extraordinary qualities of XML.

A unique feature of XML permits individual data elements to be tagged with an unlimited number of context-based definitions. Individual data elements in an XML database can then be accessed separately. In contrast the current language in general use on the Internet is hypertext markup language (HTML), which—for want of a better description—instructs a display mechanism such as a monitor or a document printer how to display data in a particular format.

The data in an HTML document cannot be separated from the format. For example, if a company were to place on its website a table in HTML showing the suggested retail prices of its various laptop models with their particular attributes such as speed and storage capacity, data in that list could be used only by displaying the information on a screen or printing it out. If a user wanted to know the median price of the company's laptops, it would be necessary to print out the table, input the data into another application, and run the numbers.

With XML, however, a program could be developed to go into the XML database, find the data for laptops, extract the prices for the machines, and compute the median price. Similarly, if a user thought that it was important to know whether the company's laptops were reasonably priced in relation to the competition, he could extract the factors considered important—say, RAM, weight, and operating speed—and develop a relationship to price that he could compare with the offerings of others.

Thus the work on what is called the Global XBRL Initiative is intended to facilitate the exchange of financial information by developing a method for translating different financial statement concepts into a common language, to be known as XBRL. This method will permit users to extract and compare information from multiple financial databases even though the information in those databases is not kept in a uniform manner (AICPA 2000b).

The XBRL Initiative is fundamentally a definitional effort. Its purpose is to seek common meanings in a common format for the various terms that companies use in maintaining their financial information. Ultimately, financial statements kept in XBRL format will be built up layer by layer from the transactional level to the composite level that is characteristic of conventional financial reports. But the format makes it possible to "drill down" into the lower levels to access the information and the judgments that were aggregated to produce the final product. The first users of this information would be company management, but it would also be possible to provide investors or analysts with limited "views" of the data that would enable them to transfer basic company data into models with which the company's value or progress could be assessed.

The advantages of this process for analyzing companies are obvious. If financial and nonfinancial information is placed in an Internet-accessible database, any user could extract the data for a unique model of how the company should be valued. Some of the data would be in XBRL form, that is, the actual transactional data that Joseph Grundfest calls "accounting primitives" (Grundfest 2000).

Other data might consist of the decisions or assumptions of management that determine the financial results ultimately reported to investors. We might assume, for example, that a company capitalizes the research and development costs for a new drug that is now ready for sale. As part of this process, the company assumes that it will recover its development costs over a six-year period and begins amortizing its capitalized costs on this basis. However, an analyst who has seen results of the drug's testing believes that it could be a major breakthrough product for the company with far more value than the company assigns. Accessing the company's financial statements—which are presented on the Internet in XBRL format—the analyst drills down to the level of financial statement aggregation and finds that the company is assuming a six-year period for recovery of development costs. Using his own model, the analyst recalculates the company's projected results with a much faster return of costs and adjusts his forecast for earnings accordingly. Through the XBRL system a user can gain access to information about a company's financial statements that would permit the development and use of the user's own model of how the company is likely to perform. Another useful category of information might be nonfinancial data elements (such as the advance purchase of raw materials or the number of research scientists) that are made available by the company without analysis or adjustment.

In theory much of the data could be made available to investors and analysts in real time, in XML format, and on the Internet. For such a program to work, however, three things are necessary: (1) the willingness of company managements to make information available, (2) the development of agreed and defined indicators that will allow companies to be compared across industries or market segments, and (3) some mechanism for verifying the accuracy of the information disclosed and the process by which it was developed. Chapter 5 discusses the incentives for management to make information available. In this chapter we discuss how such information might be made comparable and verified.

Verification of Measures and Indicators

As noted in chapter 3, the accounting profession was the first to recognize the decreasing relevance of conventional financial statements—at least for companies that rely on intangible assets for substantial portions of their value—and the need to develop alternative ways for investors to gain an understanding of company values. In a sense this is surprising since the preparation and auditing of conventional financial statements is the principal role of the accounting profession, and its acknowledgment that conventional accounting methods and statements may have to be scrapped is roughly akin to oil companies searching for alternatives to the gasoline engine.

However, leading thinkers of the accounting profession see a role for accountants even in a world in which conventional financial statements are deemphasized or replaced. This role contemplates services of two distinct kinds: (1) defining for organizations the relevant measures that will tell management how a company is meeting its objectives and giving assurance as to the reliability of the data reported in these measures (accountants refer to this function as attestation) (AICPA 1996) and (2) defining the relevant measures that will be used to compare companies with one another or to assess the value of intangible assets or the company's earning power. The latter function would include giving assurances (again as attestation) that the data reported are reliable, produced through a process that is likely to result in accurate data, and in conformity with the definitions of the measures used. For purposes of this volume, we consider only the role of accountants with respect to the second category.

The 1996 report of the AICPA's Committee on Assurance Services considers the role of auditors and the accounting profession generally in the future (AICPA 1996). In the section "Assurance on Business Performance Measures," the committee describes the services that will be performed by the CPA in assessing the accuracy of a company's business performance measures:

> The CPA assesses the reliability of the information being reported from the organization's performance measurement system (that is, are they measuring things right?). A typical system reports the actual results of an activity and compares them to an appropriate performance objective. Those results may be financial (for example, the cost of producing a product) or non-financial in nature (for example, the time it takes to produce a product). The CPA can then provide assurance as to the reliability of the information being reported. (AICPA 1996, 2)

These assurances would be sought not only by management but by investors to whom some of the business reporting measures would be disclosed. Investors would use the CPA's attestation

> to determine if management is effectively using available resources and to assist them in selecting companies for investment. If the output of an organization's performance measure-

ment system is favorable and accompanied by a report from a CPA, the entity may be able to lower financing costs and/or increase its stock price. (AICPA 1996, 4)

The attestation services of accountants will be necessary and useful in giving publicly disclosed measures and indicators credibility among investors. Somewhat surprisingly, however, the committee's report does not consider in detail the role of accountants in determining which indicators or measures should be used in particular industries. The establishment of common and uniform measures or indicators for specific industries or business segments would permit external users of this information—such as investors and analysts— to make comparisons among competing companies.

The outlines of such a service were clear in the FASB's Business Reporting Research Project: the FASB analyzed the drivers of growth in various industries that were then being reported by companies in various industries (AICPA 2000a). In addition the AICPA's Committee on Assurance Services noted in several places in its report that accountants were particularly well suited to assist individual companies in designing effective and reliable measures of business performance.[1] It is but a step from this role to working with industry groups on the design of indicators and measures that would enable cross-company comparisons within industries or across market segments.

Once these measures or indicators were designed, CPAs would be engaged not only to audit companies in the traditional sense but to attest to the quality of the systems that produced the resulting numbers. This kind of attestation would probably require less judgment and hence less legal liability than the traditional auditor's statement that a company's financial statements are a "fair presentation" of its financial position or results of operations in accordance with generally accepted accounting principles.

Real-Time Reporting

Another potential of XML and the Internet is corporate reporting of financial and nonfinancial information on a real-time basis. Since companies collect data in real time as part of the company's normal business operations, portions of the same data could theoretically be made available on the same basis. Thus daily sales could be reported as this information comes into a company's headquarters from its stores or distributors.

Although many will argue that such raw data can be misleading—that, for example, a dip in sales during a particular week might be incorrectly seen as a secular decline—there are two answers. First, investors and analysts quickly realize that such things as sales are subject to substantial variability that does not reflect long-term trends. If they fail to recognize this, they will suffer the financial consequences soon enough. Second, the models that will be used to analyze the information as it is reported will, like investors and analysts themselves, eventually be programmed to make the necessary adjustments to raw data; those that do not will fail and will be superseded by more sophisticated models.

Real-time reporting, possible only because of the existence of the Internet, is one result of the changes in technology that should cause a serious rethinking of why financial statements and other reports are issued on a periodic basis. Clearly, before the Internet, real-time reporting was not possible. Not only did assembling accurate data take time, but the data could not be disseminated immediately without great expense. The only realistic course was to publish the data in aggregated form after the agreed periods. Although this process permitted necessary adjustment—for example, the accruing of costs so that they were matched against revenues in the appropriate period—it also left the users of financial reports, such as investors, without current information until the quarterly or annual statement was published.[2]

The lack of information between periodic statements creates risk, and risk can add to volatility. Volatility and risk together increase the cost of capital for companies. That is why companies might see real-time reporting, which has now become an option, as a way to reduce their cost of capital. As the Arthur Andersen study concluded: "In the New Economy, companies will need to continuously measure and report all assets at fair value to all users" (Arthur Andersen 2000, 216).

The Prospect for the Development of Indicators

Even after the completion of the current XBRL project, the data presented in this format will be financial in nature and largely backward-looking. For XBRL to be truly useful in addressing the needs of users, it must include indicators and measures that go beyond the scope of a company's financial statements.

The development of these indicators and measures will be difficult for individual companies—and even harder if the effort is to develop indicators and measures that are common to whole industries and market segments. The problem is not insurmountable, but it must be seen as a further development of XBRL—in effect a combination of XBRL and several other efforts discussed earlier: (1) the Jenkins report's focus on user-driven and forward-looking information, (2) PwC's president's letter for Blueprint, Inc., (3) Arthur Andersen's study of value creation, (4) FASB's study of nonfinancial business reporting, (5) the management measures described in *The Balanced Scorecard* and adapted by Skandia, and (6) Baruch Lev's criteria that such measures and indicators be quantitative, standardized (or standardizable), and relevant.

As difficult as this effort will be, a strong argument can be made that it should be pressed forward. As noted by Olve, Roy, and Wetter:

> [T]he alternative—accepting the far less complete picture provided by conventional financial accounting—is certainly no better. And if we include more intangible assets in the balance sheet, we also transfer the responsibility to the person who determined their value. As far as we can see, a more detailed description, with multiple measures—in the scorecard format, for example—is the only solution. It leaves the reader free to assess the information using any model desired. (Olve, Roy, and Wetter 1999, 288)

Assuming the cooperation of companies—a major assumption discussed in chapter 5—the development of measures and indicators useful for assessing individual companies and comparing them with others is primarily a problem of definition. It would not be difficult to design in general terms the kinds of indicators that would be useful for particular industries or market segments. The truly difficult part would be defining the indicators or measures with sufficient specificity that they could be consistently applied by all companies that chose to adopt them as a basis for nonfinancial disclosure. This effort would be similar to benchmarking, a process many companies already use.[3]

The development of XBRL will provide the accounting profession and the many companies that are participants in the process with the experience of working out common definitions for financial data. This experience could be the foundation for a wider effort of this kind. It would not be completely unprecedented; groups in various industries have been working for years to define the elements of the supply chain in their industries so that manufacturers, distributors, suppliers, and resellers all use common terms for products and parts. This process, which is fundamentally the establishment of common definitions, also involves steps that would be required for the development of common financial and nonfinancial indicators.[4]

Assuming the indicators are developed, XML would also be a powerful mechanism for comparing company performance. Companies and users such as analysts could agree on indicators and measures that would be particularly useful in assessing such difficult-to-value assets as intangibles. We now know, for example, that AOL's mailout of free disks to entice customers into its system was a highly effective marketing technique. We also know that while Xerox was reaping profits from its patented copiers, it was losing the customer confidence and support that would have enabled it to hold onto its market leadership even after its patent had expired.

If AOL's success in attracting and holding new subscribers had been made plain through nonfinancial indicators, and the same data had been available for AOL's competitors at the time—a comparison made possible by the capacity of XML to harvest and compare information from different databases—an investor could have compared AOL with its rivals and perhaps realized that the company stood a good chance of dominating its market. Similarly, if the repair rates on Xerox copiers had been made available to investors, they might have been able to see that as soon as Xerox's patent ran out, its competitors would have a field day.

In this survey of the potential for financial and nonfinancial disclosure through the use of XML, we are not considering whether companies such as AOL and Xerox would have wanted their competitors to have this information. Although such disclosure is ultimately in the interest of the companies, this issue is complicated, and we discuss it further in chapter 5.

Assuming, however, that companies will make the necessary information available and will cooperate in defining the terms necessary to make the information comparable across industries or market segments, the Internet and the capabilities of XML have truly revolutionary potential for investors and analysts. The Internet has in general been a decentralizing medium, and financial analysis would be no exception. Once the necessary financial data are freed from the rigid confines of GAAP financial statements, and large amounts of nonfinancial data are also made available over the Internet, anyone with a model can access the data and can test ideas about the values of companies.

This situation is likely to give rise to a whole industry of independent analysts marketing their services to investors worldwide. Today analysts are generally employed either by the dealers who sell securities or by the large institutional investors who have the scale to pay for their services. In the future—if companies make the data available over the Internet—any investor can purchase analytical services from an independent analyst either by subscription or by viewing the advertising on the analyst's website, and this new analytical industry is likely to develop a multiplicity of models to assess the value of companies and attempt to predict their futures. The good firms will succeed in valuing companies effectively and earning the loyalty of investors. The poorly designed ones will fail. Ultimately, however, the beneficiaries of this new system will include public companies, which will find it easier to raise capital; investors, who will have access to better analysis; and the economy in general, where capital will be allocated more efficiently.

5

Encouraging Disclosure over the Internet

In January 2000 a working group of FASB's Business Reporting Research Project published its *Report of the Working Group on Electronic Distribution of Business Reporting Information* (FASB 2000). The report is remarkable for the fact that its extensive survey of business reporting on the Internet found virtually none.[1] To be sure, virtually all top 100 of the Fortune 500 companies surveyed had websites, and 93 of these companies reported some financial information on those sites. But few reported any significant amount of nonfinancial information beyond the disclosures that they were required to make in their regular annual or quarterly reports to the SEC. None included the kind of data that, for example, appeared in the supplements to the Skandia annual report.

According to the working group's survey, the material that went beyond the financial statements themselves—which were in any case frequently presented in only summary or partial form—were messages from the chairman; company, customer, or employee profiles; market outlook descriptions; vision statements; and information on share price performance. In 17 percent of the cases, however, the websites contained information that had previously been provided to analysts or links to the reports of analysts who regularly followed the company.

Companies' Concerns about Financial and Nonfinancial Disclosure

There are good reasons why companies are not disclosing more financial and nonfinancial information on the Internet. Most important, the legal liabilities associated with Internet disclosure are currently unsettled. Unlike a written and dated document, a disclosure over the Internet might be reasonably taken as a statement of current fact even though it has become out of date and hence possibly misleading. It is costly for companies to review their Internet disclosures daily to assure their continued accuracy.

Companies are justifiably afraid of investor or shareholder litigation arising out of the publication of information that is deemed misleading. This possibility can arise in a number of circumstances. Under existing securities law, a company can encounter legal liability for a disclosure that is false or for one that is true but materially misleading because it was not accompanied by other facts that were "necessary in order to make the statements made, in light of the circumstances under which they were made, not misleading" (17 C.F.R. sec. 240.10b-5—rule 10b-5). Moreover the company can be liable to investors who have sold stock on the strength of misleading information that they interpreted as negative, as well as being liable to investors who bought on the strength of misleading information that they interpreted as positive. A thorough discussion of the bases of potential liability can be found in chapter 7 of the *Report of the Working Group on Electronic Distribution of Business Reporting Information.*

In any event many companies remain wary of disclosure that goes beyond current legal requirements—and especially disclosure that might be of use to competitors. Competitive concerns might be even more important than legal concerns when companies consider whether to make the kinds of disclosures that are described in the Jenkins report and the many successor documents described in chapter 3.

Thus legal and competitive considerations provide an ample basis for companies to refuse to disclose financial or nonfinancial information, especially when no countervailing benefit seems to derive from such risks. However, it is not at all clear that these traditional objections to greater financial or nonfinancial disclosure are well founded.

The objection on the grounds of competitive disadvantage seems particularly weak. Essentially three distinct types of information might be disclosed: (1) disaggregated, raw financial data of the kind that is eventually aggregated into financial statements and would be available in XBRL format; (2) disaggregated, raw nonfinancial data that would not be included in financial statements or used in their preparation but would provide further insights for investors and others as to the value of a company; and (3) indicators or measures, whether or not used by management, that provide insight into the value, progress, or likelihood of success of a company.

Certainly some kinds of disclosure could be competitively disadvantageous. Competitors' knowledge of a company's progress in developing a particular software product could enable them to beat the innovator to market. However, not much financial data would have this effect. Even weakening sales in a particular market segment, if more than temporary, would likely be known to competitors. Companies are not wary about building, buying, or selling factories or distribution facilities, hiring or laying off workers, or making and announcing strategic alliances when these overt actions could and do alert their competitors to their strategies or their success or failure in specific areas of activity.[2]

The disclosure of disaggregated nonfinancial data might have even less of an adverse impact on competition. Information about employees as a whole (not individuals), products or services, customer retention or satisfaction, cost of customer acquisition, and employee productivity and retention may not necessarily provide a favorable picture of the company but is unlikely to give competitors information not already known through their intimate familiarity with the market. Better customer retention or lower customer-acquisition costs than those of actual or potential competitors are as likely to keep competitors out as to invite them in. And a company that does not perform well in these areas could well benefit more from seeing that improvement is possible than from revealing its weakness to its competitors.

If a company decides to make measures or indicators available unilaterally—and not as part of any agreed industrywide disclosure program—it could design the measures in such a way as to ensure that competitively useful information is not made available. The same would be true of an industrywide disclosure program since the measures and indicators would have to be designed and agreed by the participants. During the design process the indicators could be structured to limit the competitively useful information conveyed. Many measures and indicators in *The Balanced Scorecard* (see chapter 3), though useful to management, would not necessarily be harmful if disclosed to competitors.

The possibility that disclosures could have significant adverse legal consequences is in many ways a more difficult problem for management than that of adverse competitive results. For one thing the competitive consequences are easier for management to isolate and weigh than the possibility of a lawsuit based on facts or conditions that may come to light only later. For another, legal outcomes can be much less certain than competitive outcomes; judges and juries are unpredictable, and a serious legal threat takes management away from the task of managing the business, while a competitive threat intensifies management's involvement with the company's business.

Conversely, of the three different disclosures being discussed here, only the third—disclosure of currently nontraditional measures or indicators—seems to provide a reasonable basis for legal liability. It is difficult to see how the availability of underlying financial data in the XBRL format—assuming it is accurate—can be deemed in any way misleading. And while disaggregated or raw nonfinancial information could be deemed to have this affect, the Private Securities Litigation Reform Act of 1995 (15 U.S.C. sec. 77z) provides companies with a strong defense against liability for the publication of facts that are accurate reflections of their records.

For all disclosures to which rule 10b-5 is applicable—including both disaggregated financial and nonfinancial information—the law requires that a plaintiff prove that the company acted either deliberately with intent to deceive or recklessly in publishing the allegedly misleading information. It would be difficult for a plaintiff to prove that a company's publication of true financial or nonfinancial information could have been done with intent to deceive. Although the courts have not set a clear standard of recklessness, it would also be difficult for a plaintiff to argue that a true statement of fact concerning financial or nonfinancial data was published recklessly.

Certain indicators or measures, such as ratios, that go beyond raw numbers themselves could be deemed materially misleading and consequently that their publication would be reckless or done with intent to deceive. In particular, companies that disclose indicators or measures of their own devising—especially if they do not reveal how the measures were developed or what facts were omitted—could be subject to legal liability. But it would be difficult if not impossible to make a case for recklessness against a company that published accurate information in accordance with measures or indicators that were defined in advance by industry groups or competitors in market segments. Accordingly, while there is opposition to disclosure of financial and nonfinancial data among companies because of concern about competitive disadvantage or legal liability, these worries seem considerably overblown.

Why Companies Should Disclose

But it is still not clear why any company would want to publish such material—why, in other words, it should take any risk or incur any expense to make these data available to investors and analysts. Companies might find this course attractive for several good reasons.

First, as noted in chapter 3, conventional financial statements do not provide sufficient information concerning a company's prospects to be of great value to investors. Increasingly these reports are becoming irrelevant to an accurate valuation of knowledge companies and others. High levels of uncertainty and market volatility increase investor risk and the risk premiums that investors demand, which in turn raise companies' cost of capital.

In a 1994 article entitled "Costs and Benefits of Business Information Disclosure," Robert K. Elliott and Peter D. Jacobson describe this process as follows:

> The ideal, minimum cost of capital is the risk-free rate of return plus the premium for economic risk. However, the only way the investor or creditor can assess economic risk is through information.... As the company provides more informative disclo-

sure, the demanded rates decline, because the capital supplier has a better and better understanding of the enterprise's economic risk.... Thus when the information indicates poor prospects, it means that the economic risk premium is high, not that the information is functioning to raise the cost of capital. Ignorance of a company's risks (the highest level of information risk premium) is still an increment above the risk-free rate of return plus the economic premium. Getting a better understanding of the true economic risk would still lower the cost of capital. (81–82)

A company that can reduce uncertainty concerning its value and can establish a stable market price based on credible information about its operations is likely to reduce its cost of capital. One of the studies cited earlier in chapter 5 confirms what one would expect—that increased disclosure reduces capital costs. In that study Christine Botosan of Washington University reviewed a sample of 122 manufacturing firms in an attempt to determine whether there was a relationship between the amount of disclosure in their 1990 annual reports and their capital costs. She concluded:

> For firms that attract a low analyst following, the results indicate that greater disclosure is associated with a lower cost of equity capital. The magnitude of the effect is such that a one-unit difference in the disclosure measure is associated with a difference of approximately 28 basis points in the cost of equity capital, after controlling for market beta and firm size. For firms with a high analyst following, however, I find no evidence of an association between my measure of disclosure level and the cost of equity capital perhaps because the disclosure measure is limited to the annual report and accordingly may not provide a powerful proxy for overall disclosure level when analysts play a significant role in the communication process.[3] (Botosan 1997, 323)

Botosan's study compared the specific nonfinancial disclosures of the companies reviewed and then awarded points for each disclosure of information not required in the financial statements or obtainable from the financial statements. She found a good deal of variation between companies:

Cascade Corporation's disclosure score of 12.0 marks the first percentile of the distribution. In its 1990 annual report, Cascade Corporation provides no discussion of its principal products or markets and presents a very limited, five year summary of historical results. The only key non-financial statistic disclosed is the number of individuals employed by the company, and no forecast information is included in the report. Its management discussion and analysis discusses the change in its sales, net income, capital expenditures and market share in qualitative terms only. (Botosan 1997, 334)

The company at the opposite end of the scale, Cummins Engine, received a score of 46—reflecting almost four times more disclosure than Cascade:

Cummins' report provides a detailed discussion of its principal products and markets with specific quantitative information, a comprehensive ten year summary of historical results and several key non-financial statistics such as number of employees, average compensation per employee, market share statistics and units sold. In addition, Cummins' management discussion and analysis deals with more items than Cascade's and incorporates quantitative information not recoverable from the financial statements and footnotes. Finally, Cummins' report includes profit and sales projections, a discussion of the future impact of existing industry trends, and a capital expenditure budget for the year. (Botosan 1997, 334)

Although Botosan does not provide a number that reflects the difference between the capital costs of Cummins and Cascade, we can assume from her general conclusions, as quoted above, that the difference was considerable, even controlling for elements that might affect capital costs.

Another cause of uncertainty and volatility is the periodic nature of corporate financial disclosure. In general, corporations report their financial results quarterly on an unaudited basis (though with accountant review far short of an audit) and report their annual financial results with an audited report shortly after the end of their fiscal years. Between quarterly reports the securities market is subject to rumors about the condition of particular companies or industries, rumors that occasionally cause sharp changes in the values of equity securities. This problem has grown more severe with the advent of the Internet, which permits rumors to spread rapidly through chat rooms and day traders to buy or sell on a momentum theory.

At the same time company managers fear the consequences of surprising the market at the end of a quarter or a year. This concern may be so great that they seek to manage earnings to meet market expectations, a matter that has drawn the attention of the SEC chairman. Again volatility caused by uncertainty between financial reports increases investors' perceived risks and thus tends to increase the cost of capital. Uncertainty caused by investors' concern that earnings are being managed and do not accurately reflect a company's real results has the same effect.

These problems would be reduced or eliminated by real-time disclosure of basic financial or nonfinancial data, including various measures and indicators used by management or agreed within an industry. Because of the communication capabilities of the Internet, disclosure of this information does not have to occur periodically. To the extent that adjustment is necessary because of seasonal or other factors, the models of the analysts will do this without company intervention. Recall that Arthur Andersen, in *Cracking the Value Code*, expressed the view that continuous measurement and reporting would become the gold standard for companies in the future.

Third, companies that make the most disclosures of the most meaningful and informative data and measures should gain a substantial advantage in raising capital against competitors and others who do not. To the extent that well-managed and successful companies can differentiate themselves from less well-managed competitors through information disclosure, they will increase their competitive advantage or achieve an advantage that they had not been able to gain in other areas. Here disclosure can provide a competitive advantage instead of the disadvantage that some companies fear.

As outlined in the Arthur Andersen report:

[W]e think the premium for openness (or transparency) is going to rise dramatically in the coming years. Research shows that reporting more to investors and other stakeholders than is required under law can benefit an organization. We are already seeing investors, customers, employees, and other partners flocking to those companies that are providing the best information for informed decision-making. Companies that gain a reputation for openness are likely to find a market more forgiving of occasional bad news. Investors will reward such openness by reducing the rate of return they require from a company, thereby lowering the company's cost of capital. (2000, 227)

These factors, and especially the last one, should cause disclosure to increase through the operation of the market alone, without government intervention. Significant government intervention—say, in the form of mandating certain required disclosure—is likely to be counterproductive, however. Government standard setting tends to establish a ceiling—an acceptable standard—that discourages innovation. As has become true with conventional financial statements and the management discussion and analysis required by the SEC in various disclosure documents, few companies believe that they need to go beyond what the SEC has required.

Our view, in agreement with many members of the accounting profession, is that the market will bestow a sufficiently great advantage on companies that are open and informative to make better disclosure the rule rather than the exception.[4] There is considerable incentive for managements to do so, beginning with companies that will be able to benefit from disclosure and gradually extending to their competitors. As investors come to expect greater disclosure, companies that fail to meet the standard will be increasingly penalized.

Government in the Disclosure Process

But government does have an important role—one as catalyst. Thus far the pace of change in developing and implementing a new model of corporate disclosure has been slow, and government should have a strong interest in speeding it up for several reasons.

First, investors would be better informed—a key objective of the SEC. Not only would investors have more information with which to make judgments about the allocation of their resources among companies, but their information would improve in quality. In light of the deteriorating usefulness of conventional accounting reports (Lev and Zarowin 1999), nonfinancial data would assist investors in forecasting the future of potential investments, and in the case of knowledge companies and others with large amounts of intangible assets, these data would enable investors to assess the value of intangibles to a greater extent than is possible through the analysis of conventional financial statements.

Second, as noted, the widespread availability of nonfinancial data on the Internet—data that have probative worth regarding the value and prospects of companies—would likely encourage the development of a whole industry of independent analysts with competing models for using the newly accessible data. The decentralization of analysts' services—away from sell-side broker-dealers or buy-side institutional investors—would provide investors with greater assistance in making their own investment judgments than is true in today's market.

Third, the greater availability of information should, as noted above, reduce volatility in the markets and increase investor confidence in corporate values (Lev 2000). Fourth, if, as some fear, the historically high levels of market capitalization suggest that a bubble has developed, it is at least in part the result of a deficiency of high-quality information about the current condition of companies. Encouraging companies to make disclosures of nonfinancial information, accessible over the Internet, will either confirm the high expectations of investors or bring company capital values down to realistic levels and reduce the likelihood that bubbles will develop.

Fifth, the chairman of the SEC has recently expressed concern about the possibility that companies are managing their earnings to conform to the expectations of analysts and are managing the expectations of analysts to encourage earnings forecasts that the companies can meet. If so, investors are receiving even less useful information than normally supplied by conventional financial statements. This situation can happen because financial reports are periodic reports issued quarterly and annually (FASB 2000). Many financial and nonfinancial indicators and measures that will be developed or made accessible over the Internet will be available in real time, will allow analysts and investors to get a better picture of events between financial reports, and will make surprises less likely. Since avoiding surprises is the principal purpose of earnings management, company officials will feel less need to manage the expectations of the market as a periodic report approaches.

Finally, the availability of better information concerning companies should facilitate the allocation of capital in our economy—certainly a matter that should be an overriding concern of government.

Under these circumstances we should expect government—primarily the SEC—to take some role in encouraging the improvement and upgrading of the information made available to investors. The accounting profession—through XBRL—is well along in the process of preparing financial information for wide distribution over the Internet. Various accounting firms are beginning to educate their clients about the benefits of what PwC calls *ValueReporting* and Arthur Andersen calls *Cracking the Value Code.*

As noted, there are also good reasons why private companies will want to make more financial and nonfinancial information available to investors and good reasons to believe that the fears of those who oppose more disclosure are either unfounded or can be overcome with careful design. Accordingly the role for government and specifically the SEC may be only a limited one—bringing the necessary parties together, encouraging discussion, acknowledging the benefits for investors and the economy generally. Given the incentives for disclosure, more than this may not be necessary.

The OECD appears to be heading in this direction. In an effort to explore, understand, and communicate how companies generate intangible value, the OECD has established a Public-Private Forum on Value Creation in the Knowledge Economy. In announcing the forum, the OECD noted that the program would rely on voluntary reporting and continued: "[I]ndividual companies have made considerable progress in identifying, measuring and reporting on intangible assets and their role in value creation. However, if such information is to be a useful complement to financial data, it needs to be more comparable and verifiable" (OECD 2000).

As Robert G. Eccles wrote in *Measuring Corporate Performance,* a publication of the *Harvard Business Review,* the opposition to disclosure is likely to be overcome without government action:

> Ultimately, a regulatory body like the SEC could untie this Gordian knot by recommending (and eventually requiring) public companies to provide nonfinancial measures in their reports. (This is, after all, how financial standards became so omnipotent and why so many millions of hours have been invested in their development.) But I suspect competitive pressure will prove a more immediate force for change. As soon as one leading company can demonstrate the long-term advantage of its superior performance on quality or innovation or any other non-financial measure, it will change the rules for all its rivals forever. And with so many serious competitors tracking—and enhancing—these measures, that is only a matter of time. (1991, 42)

These words were written in 1991, and it is appropriate to ask why the changes Eccles predicts have not yet come about. There is no easy answer. But clearly the intervening years have demonstrated a growing need for a system of disclosure that goes beyond conventional financial statements and the limited commentary required for a company's MD&A.

The advent of the Internet has introduced a communications medium that would permit the dissemination of financial and nonfinancial information virtually without cost; the development of XBRL shows the way to using the unique qualities of XML to mine and analyze data; and industry efforts like RosettaNet to define the elements of the supply chain in XML format demonstrate that cooperation among competitors is possible and beneficial for the industries involved. Someone—preferably the private sector, but the government if necessary—needs to kick start the process of developing better disclosure for investors.

Notes

Chapter 1
The Importance and the Direction of Disclosure

1. The basic discounted dividend (or earnings) model of corporate stock price valuation was developed by John Williams (1938) decades ago.

Chapter 2
A Backward Look at
Disclosure Practices and Conventions

1. The discussion in this section is based on Previts and Merino (1998).

2. The state of New York enacted a statute in 1848 that required companies to publish information about their financial accounts but did not prescribe any methods for doing so.

3. Initially the disclosure requirements applied only to companies whose shares were listed on the major exchanges. In 1964 Congress extended the requirements to shares that were traded over the counter.

4. For a more complete discussion of this subject, see Gephardt 2000.

5. See Botosan 1997 (voluntary disclosure lowers the equity cost of capital for firms not widely followed by financial analysts); Sengupta 1998 (more disclosure leads to lower cost of debt); Heal, Hutton, and Palepu 2000 (more disclosure is positively correlated with subsequent stock performance and degree of institutional ownership).

6. Liability can exist under sections 10b-5, 11, and 12(a)(2) of the Securities Act of 1933. In different ways each section exposes companies, their officers and directors, and their accountants to liability for misleading statements.

Chapter 3
Corporate Disclosure in the Knowledge Economy

1. Katherine Schipper, in the background paper prepared for this project, takes a different view. She argues that empirical research indicates an increasingly strong statistical association over time between corporate book values and share prices. However, the statistical work on which this conclusion is based runs only through the year 1994, when average stock prices were less than half the levels at the time this monograph was prepared.

2. This is based on calculations from chapter 3 of PricewaterhouseCoopers, forthcoming.

3. This is not a new idea. In a supplement to its annual report for 1994, Skandia International Insurance Corporation, a Swedish insurer that has been a leader in the field of developing indicators of intangible values, stated:

> Many Swedish companies on the Stockholm Stock Exchange are valued at 3–8 times their book value, i.e., the financial capital. In the U.S. the corresponding valuation is often higher. This implies that there will be huge hidden values in such companies that are not visible in the traditional accounting. Yet it is precisely these hidden areas—from an accounting viewpoint—in which major investments for the future are made. Such intangible investments concern customer relationships, information technology, networks and employees' competence. (Skandia 1994, 5)

4. See, for example, papers presented at the OECD International Symposium on Measuring and Reporting Intellectual Capital: Experience, Issues, and Prospects, Amsterdam, June 9–11, 1999 (OECD 2000). Among the chairman's conclusions: "The process of value creation in companies is changing. There is a need for better information on intellectual capital, its relation to tangible capital, and its role in value creation. Financial data are evolving, but, alone, present insufficient information."

5. As Paul Strassmann (1999) has noted:

Unfortunately, the attempts to assign a valuation to software assets, trademarks, experience and employee know-how have run so far into the difficult problem of pricing such assets. It is now widely understood that the costs of acquiring knowledge and the profit-generation potentials of such knowledge are unrelated. The value of intellectual property is in its use, not its costs. This means that they are only worth what a customer is willing to pay for.

6. To a substantial degree, this is the issue in the current debate over purchase compared with pooling accounting in the case of mergers. Purchase accounting permits accountants to place a value on the intangible assets of a company that has been purchased for an amount in excess of the depreciated value of its tangible assets. The excess value is considered goodwill and is written off against the acquired company's earnings over a specified period. Is this better accounting than allowing the two companies to pool their assets without seeking to establish a value for the intangible assets of either? As usual the answer depends on how one views some additional factors in the equation. Among them are the question whether even the purchase price for the acquired company establishes a fair value for its intangible assets and whether it is fair to value the intangible assets of an acquired company in this way—just because it was involved in an acquisition transaction—when the intangibles of an identical company that has not been acquired would be treated differently. Golub (2000) shows that a merged company made up of two identical American Express companies would have different profit results if the merger were treated as a purchase rather than a pooling. But this demonstration simply raises the question whether—in the absence of the capitalization and subsequent depreciation of their intangible assets—the profits of each of the constituent companies were fairly presented before the merger. Finally, in purchase accounting, if the price paid for assets exceeds their cost basis, the difference is designated "goodwill" and written off over some reasonable period. But if the goodwill items are intangibles, they do not necessarily depreciate, and they may have a useful life that extends well beyond the life of tan-

gible assets. In those circumstances amortizing goodwill may not make sense or reflect reality.

7. Ironically, in May 2000 AOL settled a dispute with the SEC over the capitalization of its customer-acquisition costs between 1994 and 1996. The company paid a civil fine of $3.5 million without admitting any wrongdoing.

8. That volatility has increased is based on the authors' discussion with G. William Schwert of Rochester University, updating his 1998 study, "Stock Market Volatility: Ten Years after the Crash" (Schwert 2000).

9. In addition to market volatility, inadequate information about a major component of a company's value has other consequences. Specially informed or particularly knowledgeable investors can reap abnormally high profits because of their information advantage. A company's management may have an even greater than normal advantage over outsiders if they are the only ones with significant information about the company's intangible assets. Even professional analysts may be at a disadvantage in relation to specially informed investors if they cannot derive relevant data about intangibles from the company's published reports. This information asymmetry will also cause spreads in the markets to increase as market-makers realize that there is information about a company that may be held by especially informed investors with whom they are required to trade. Widening spreads are a way for market-makers to reduce their risks in an information-poor environment.

10. Baruch Lev (2000) supports this point:

> The traditional business model of an introverted, somewhat secretive enterprise, interacting with outsiders mainly through exchanges of property rights (sales, purchases, financial investments) is reasonably well accounted for by traditional, transaction-based accounting. Such an inward-oriented business model is quickly giving way to an open, extroverted model, where important relationships with customers, suppliers and even competitors are not fully characterized by property right exchanges.

11. Benchmarking is a process by which companies improve their performance by studying the best practices of others. This

involves qualitative studies of particular cases or quantitative comparisons in a group of organizations with commonly agreed measurements

Chapter 4
The Way Forward

1. See, for example, AICPA 1996, 2. For organizations that do not have performance measurement systems, the services of CPAs can include "helping design and implement a performance measurement system."

2. The Arthur Andersen study (2000, 225–26) quotes former SEC commissioner Stephen M. H. Wallman for this proposition:

> "Businesses are run on a continuous basis," [Wallman] recently told an audience. Without "the artificiality of the quarterly reporting system," activities "like trying to move inventory at the end of a certain quarter in order to show an uptick in revenues" would disappear. "Analysts and investors," Wallman went on, "would judge a stock based on a company's performance and prospects, not on how well it manages a certain number four times a year."

3. Since 1991, the American Society for Training and Development has sponsored a benchmarking program on employee education and training in which many Fortune 500 companies participate. The work of the program was described as follows by Laurie J. Bassie, vice president for research of ASTD, in a statement to the OECD conference "Measuring and Reporting Intellectual Capital" in June 1999: "The work in the early years of the Benchmarking Forum consisted of painstaking efforts to reach agreement among firms representing very different industries with regard to a common set of definitions and metrics.... It took until 1995 for these efforts to stabilize into a measurement methodology that was acceptable, feasible, and useful to members." The ASTD has also begun a program to develop a comprehensive set of intellectual capital indicators. The participants, according to Bassie, have agreed "on a core set of intellectual capital

indicators that, in their view, have broad applicability and are feasible to collect" (Bassie 1999).

4. One example of the current work going on in industry is RosettaNet.org, an organization of the electronic components and information technologies industries, which is engaged in establishing common definitions—in effect a dictionary—for the many items in the supply chains of these two industries. Once these definitions have been established, manufacturers could seek parts and components from a broader array of suppliers on a global basis, and suppliers could have a better sense of whether they can meet the needs of manufacturers and distributors.

Chapter 5
Encouraging Disclosure over the Internet

1. This is to be distinguished from the findings of the working groups that were studying the disclosures in particular industries. These numerous disclosures were written in annual reports and other disclosure documents.

2. In *Performance Drivers* (1999), Olve, Roy, and Wetter comment on the view that the information in a company's balanced scorecard—information used by management to assess whether the company is meeting its objectives—would be far more valuable to competitors than the company's internal accounting information:

> [T]he situation is no different in principle when companies invest in certain countries, hire certain researchers, or build factories for a certain type of production. The only difference is that these actions are more visible. And potential financiers (via the stock exchange or in other ways) should also have an opportunity to decide whether they want to help the company invest in software, training, new products, or any other intangible assets. (291)

3. The average sample firm was followed by approximately eleven analysts. The lower quartile was followed by an average of five analysts, and the upper quartile by fifteen.

4. Baruch Lev concurs and notes that there is an important reason for narrowing what he calls the "company investors perception gap":

> An undervaluation of a company's equity or excessive volatility of stock price implies that its *cost of capital* is unduly high. Not only will a new stock issue under such circumstances be expensive to float, but any other form of financing (bank loan, bond issue) will be costly too, given the strong interrelationships among the various segments of the capital market. (emphasis in the original) (Lev nd)

References

American Institute of Certified Public Accountants. 2000a. *Improving Business Reporting—A Customer Focus (the Jenkins Report)*. http://www.aicpa.org/members/div/accstd/ibr/appiv.htm. February 21.

————. 2000b. Press release, April 6. http://www.aicpa.org/news/p040600.htm.

————. Special Committee on Assurance Services. 1996. *Assurance on Business Performance Measures. Report of the Special Committee.* (Ellicott report.) http://www.aicpa.org/assurance/scas/newvs./perf/index.htm.

Arthur Andersen. 2000. *Cracking the Value Code.* HarperBusiness.

Bassie, Laurie J. 1999. Statement presented at Organization for Economic Cooperation and Development symposium "Measuring and Reporting Intellectual Capital." Amsterdam.

Botosan, Christine A. 1997. "Disclosure Level and the Cost of Equity Capital." *Accounting Review* 72 (3) (July): 323.

Council of Economic Advisers. 2000. *Economic Report of the President, 2000,* pp. 79–83. Washington, D.C.: Government Printing Office.

Eccles, Robert G. 1991. "The Performance Measurement Manifesto." *In Measuring Corporate Performance.* Boston: Harvard Business School Press. (reprinted in 1998).

Elliott, Robert K. 1992. "The Third Wave Breaks on the Shores of Accounting." *Accounting Horizons* 6 (2) (June): 61–85.

Elliott, Robert K., and Peter D. Jacobson. 1994. "Costs and Benefits of Business Information Disclosure." *Accounting Horizons* 8 (4): 81–82.

Financial Accounting Standards Board. 2000. *Report of the Working Group on Electronic Distribution of Business Reporting Information.* http://www.fasb.org.

————. Food Industry Working Group. No date. *Business Reporting Research Project.* Draft.

————. 1999. *Business Reporting Research Project: Summary.*

Gephardt, Gunther. 2000. "The Evolution of Global Standards in Accounting." In *Brookings-Wharton Papers on Financial Services*, edited by Robert E. Litan and Anthony M. Sentomero. Washington, D.C.: Brookings.

Glassman, James K., and Kevin A. Hassett. 1999. *Dow 36,000.* New York: Random House.

Golub, Harvey. 2000. Testimony before Senate Banking Committee, March 2.

Grundfest, Joseph A. 2000. "Corporate Disclosure in the Internet Age." Paper delivered at AEI-Brookings Joint Center on Regulatory Studies conference.

Heal, Paul, Amy Hutton, and Krishna Palepu. 2000. "Stock Performance and Intermediation Changes surrounding Sustained Increases in Disclosure." Unpublished manuscript. Cambridge. Harvard Business School.

Hunt, Margaret. 1989. "Time-Management, Writing, and Accounting in the Eighteenth-Century English Trading Family: A Bourgeois Enlightenment." *Business and Economic History,* vol. 18. 2nd. series, p. 155.

Kaplan, Robert S., and David P. Norton. 1996. *The Balanced Scorecard.* Boston: Harvard Business School Press.

Leadbeater, Charles. 1999. "New Measures for the New Economy." Paper presented at the Organization of Economic Cooperation and Development symposium "Measuring and Reporting Intellectual Capital." Amsterdam.

Lev, Baruch. 2000. *Intangibles.* Draft of forthcoming book from the Brookings Institution.

————. No date. "Communicating Knowledge Capabilities."

Lev, Baruch, and Paul Zarowin. 1999. "The Boundaries of Financial Reporting and How to Extend Them." February.

Olve, Nils-Goran, Jan Roy, and Magnus Wetter. 1999. *Performance Drivers.* New York: John Wiley.

Organization for Economic Cooperation and Development. 2000. "Public-Private Forum on Value Creation in the Knowledge

Economy—Overview." http://www.oecd.org/daf/corporate affairs/ disclosure/intangibles.htm.

Previts, Gary John, and Barbara Dubis Merino. 1998. *A History of Accounting in the United States.* Columbus: Ohio State University Press.

PricewaterhouseCoopers. 1999. *ValueReporting Forecast 2000.*

———. Forthcoming. *The Value Reporting Revolution: Moving Beyond the Earnings Game.* New York: Wiley.

Schwert, G. William. 2000. "Stock Market Volatility: Ten Years after the Crash." In *Brookings-Wharton Papers on Financial Services,* edited by Robert E. Litan and Anthony M. Sentomero. Washington, D.C.: Brookings.

Sengupta, Partha. 1998. "Corporate Disclosure Quality and the Cost of Debt." *Accounting Review* 73 (4).

Shiller, Robert. 2000. *Irrational Exuberance.* Princeton: Princeton University Press.

Skandia. 1994. *Visualizing Intellectual Capital in Skandia.* Supplement to Skandia's 1994 annual report. www.skandia.com/capital/supplements.htm.

———. 1995. *Value Creating Processes.* Supplement to Skandia's 1995 annual report. www.skandia.com/capital/supplements.htm.

———. 1998. *Human Capital in Tranformation: Intellectual Capital Prototype Report.* www.skandia.com/capital/supplements.htm.

Strassmann, Paul. 1999. *Measuring and Managing Knowledge Capital.* Knowledge Executive Report, June.

Summers, Lawrence. 2000. "Distinguished Lecture on Economics in Government: Reflections on Managing Global Integration." *Journal of Economic Perspectives* 13 (2) (spring): 3–18.

Williams, John B. 1938. *The Theory of Investment Value.* Cambridge: Harvard University Press.

About the Authors

ROBERT E. LITAN is the vice president and the director of the Economic Studies Program and Cabot Family Chair in Economics at the Brookings Institution. He is also the codirector of the AEI-Brookings Joint Center on Regulatory Studies; the coeditor of the *Brookings-Wharton Papers on Financial Services* and *Emerging Markets Finance* (with the World Bank and International Monetary Fund); and the cochairman of the Shadow Financial Regulatory Committee. He is both an economist and an attorney.

During 1995 and 1996 Mr. Litan was the associate director, Office of Management and Budget. From 1993 to 1995 he was the deputy assistant attorney general, Department of Justice. From 1977 to 1979 he was the regulatory and legal staff specialist at the President's Council of Economic Advisers.

Recently Mr. Litan cowrote a congressionally mandated baseline study for the Treasury Department on the role of the Community Reinvestment Act after the Financial Modernization Act of 1999. During 1996–1997 he was a consultant to the Treasury Department on its report to Congress on the future of the financial services industry; in 1998–1999 he was the main author of the *Report of the President's Commission to Study Capital Budgeting*. In 1998 he was the chairman of the National Academy of Sciences Committee on Assessing the Costs of Natural Disasters.

Mr. Litan has written, cowritten, and edited twenty books and more than 125 articles on government policies on financial institutions, regulatory and legal issues, international trade, and the economy. His most recent books include *Globaphobia: Confronting Fears about Open Trade* (with Gary Burtless, Robert Lawrence, and Robert Shapiro); *Going Digital!* (with William Niskanen); *American Finance for the Twenty-First Century* (with Jonathan Rauch); and *None of Your Business: World Data Flows and the European Privacy Directive* (with

Peter Swire). He is codirecting, with Alice Rivlin, a project on the economic impact of the Internet.

PETER J. WALLISON joined the American Enterprise Institute for Public Policy Research in January 1999 as codirector of AEI's program on financial market deregulation. He had practiced banking, corporate, and financial law in Washington, D.C., and New York. From June 1981 to January 1985 Mr. Wallison was the general counsel of the Treasury Department and the general counsel to the Depository Institutions Deregulation Committee. During 1986 and 1987 he was the counsel to President Ronald Reagan. Between 1972 and 1976 Mr. Wallison was a special assistant to Nelson A. Rockefeller while he was the governor of New York and then the counsel to Mr. Rockefeller when he was the vice president of the United States.

Mr. Wallison is the author of *Back from the Brink,* a structure for a private deposit insurance system, and the coauthor of *Nationalizing Mortgage Risk: The Growth of Fannie Mae and Freddie Mac,* both published by AEI; he has written numerous articles for banking publications. He is also the editor of *Optional Federal Chartering and Regulation of Insurance Companies,* also published by AEI. Mr. Wallison is a member of the Shadow Financial Regulatory Committee and the Council on Foreign Relations.

J O I N T C E N T E R